a royal anglian

The memoirs of a squaddie, 1975-86

Mark Eagle

Continue..

A ROYAL ANGLIAN

ISBN:9781699034439

First published in Great Britain in 2019

Copyright ©2019

Mark Eagle has asserted his right under the Copyright Designs and Patents Act 1988 to be identified as the author of this work.

A CIP catalogue record for this book is available from the British Library. This book is sold subject to the condition that it shall not by way of trade or otherwise be lent, resold, hired out or otherwise circulated without the publisher's prior consent in any form of binding or cover, other than that in which it is published and without a similar condition, including this condition being imposed on the subsequent purchaser.

Typeset in 9/12pt Bembo

Continue..

Contents

	Preface	
Chapter 1	The kid from Rothwell	1
Chapter 2	You're in the Army now	9
Chapter 3	Passing out	23
Chapter 4	Cyprus and the UN	33
Chapter 5	Into the Troubles	53
Chapter 6	Colchester, 1979-84	77
Chapter 7	Kenya, 1980	90
Chapter 8	Belize, 1982	100
Chapter 9	USA, 1984	106
Chapter 10	Germany, 1984	121
Chapter 11	Exercise Lionheart	134
Chapter 12	Civvy Street	152

Continue..

Preface

This story is focused on my military career, from the start in Rothwell, Northamptonshire, to the present day. Where possible I have split the book into sections for the different postings or theatres in chronological order, to the best of my knowledge and memory. I have taken memories or events and stories from each one, with the aim of giving as much detail as possible. At the end of the book I have included a glossary of military terminology. I have used the odd swear word where it was needed. The names of all the people mentioned are real, though abbreviated.

Continue..

CHAPTER 1

The kid from Rothwell

Before I continue, I shall give you an insight as to life as it was before I joined the Army in September 1975. I grew up in Rothwell, a small Northamptonshire town about five miles from Kettering and twenty miles from Northampton. Rothwell is a rural Midland town surrounded by gently rolling hills and country lanes, with a population of around 15,000 souls. It has a mixture of mainly terraced council housing and new developments popping up of quite modern two, three or sometimes four-bedroom houses and of course a scattering of farmhouses and working farms in the area. It was a small town where everyone knew each other, and it was always good to keep up with the local gossip. It was a nice village-sized town in the heart of Northamptonshire, where everybody knew each other pretty much and life was good. There was a decency among the people that is rare today. A neighbour would bring your washing in from the clothes line if they noticed that rain had started falling, and there was no need for locked doors – people were trustworthy, and respect was shown to adults and especially the elderly.

I had a normal and I suppose average school life, with not too many friends, but I lived for football, day and night and at weekends. We played whether it was sun, rain, hail or snow. We also would build our own cycles, all second-hand of course, but I do remember getting a now highly sought-after Chopper bike for Christmas – some surprise that was, believe me, as there wasn't much money around for expensive toys or bikes then. We would also build our own 'soap boxes', or 'go carts' I think we called them then.

On leaving school most lads would usually go to one of the many boot and shoe factories in the area. Northamptonshire was famed for them back then, but there are not so many of them now. The two names that stand out are, or were, Groococks and Clarks.

We were taught how to tell right from wrong, and we learned respect, manners and discipline. We were a large family, so there was always something going on at home. We were not well off, but Mum always managed to get us through. There were seven of us in total at this time, five boys and two girls, and I was the fourth eldest.

Mum and Dad split up when I was around nine years old. He used to visit every couple of weeks, but this petered out as we grew older. Mum got together with a guy named Brian, and they stayed together until she passed away, maybe a year after. Sadly, after that Brian took his own life; my brother Richard found him. He had changed a lot since losing Mum, and the doctors said he just missed her too much and could not face life without her. My brothers and I would try and get him out for a drink, but he lost interest in that too. He was a decent man and a good stepfather to us all.

At school I was average I guess, certainly not stupid. I missed the last six months on and off to look after Mum after she had a bad fall. I had to take care of the house and generally do everything she could not at age 15. I could count my few friends on one hand. I wasn't a drinker, as I preferred to keep fit. I had a girlfriend or two, but nothing too serious as we were still just kids. It was all part of the growing up process, I suppose.

So, it was football in the Mounts, a small park where we all used to gather for football, my biggest love at this time, bikes and general messing about. We played football morning, noon and night, and believe me we played some excellent games. I recall one time when the men from the local foundry works next to the park came over and took us on, boys against men, but they did not have a chance – we were pretty good back then. We used to go almost every week to watch Rothwell Town on Saturday, plus we had our own local team –

Jubilee Street Rovers was the name, I think. We had a manager and played on Sundays. I remember once the team having its result in the Pink Paper, a local rag for the sports, and was fantastic to see. I'm sure it read Jubilee Street Rovers 2, Whoever 0. I wasn't a bad player either, on the wing à la George Best, and like all kids I wanted to be a professional.

There was never much excitement around,

and by the age of sixteen I was looking to escape. I didn't get the chance though. I got a job as an apprentice welder at a small garage on the A6, now a McDonalds. It was a small family-run business and they were good, honest hard-working people. Electric arc welding was my job and I enjoyed it to some extent, but it was going to take time to qualify, and I would have needed to study. I hope you get the feel of the place we called home.

One of the low points of those early years was the death of my brother Steven – we shared the same bedroom at home. Steven was a quiet lad, well-mannered and a wizard for all things electrical – he must have got this knowledge from our Dad, a television engineer. He would love the technology of today and would have made a computer programmer or something similar. Steve and I were both smokers and would very often pool our resources for a packet of five Park Drive tipped. Mostly of course the cheap option was tobacco and papers.

Steve wasn't a sporty type like me, he was more hands-on and was very clever with all thing electrical. He would be in our bedroom for hours stripping down old transistor radios and rebuilding them with better reception and sound. He would play Radio

Caroline, if I remember correctly. He would have loved the technology of today and I would imagine that he would have become a game developer or some such career.

Bedroom space was at a premium with two sisters and five brothers crammed into a mid-terrace house, but we managed it. However, in the room Steve and I had the bed was tight to the bedroom door, so we could not open it fully as his bed was directly behind it. He was smoking in bed and fell asleep – need I say more? All I can remember is the fire engines and plenty of screaming, shouting and crying. I think the local doctor gave us all a sleeping pill or something. It was a terrible night, and it will stay with all of us forever.

I was fourteen when Steven died. Obviously the house was fire damaged and the council decided to put us all in the Rothwell House Hotel. The details are sketchy but I'm sure we were there for a couple of months. We finally got re-housed in Meadow Road.

Anyway, Steven is on my mind on a daily basis and I will never forget about him. I drive past Jubilee Street regularly and think of him almost every day,

how he would have. As I mentioned before, I am sure he would have made a career in the electrical business, even another inventor like James Dyson perhaps. I hope there is something afterwards, because I so want to see him again and tell him how I missed him. We were close and he was a really calm type of person, a cool dude really. It was great to share the room with him. If there is such a place as Heaven I am certain he will be responsible for lighting the place up!

Our weeks at Rothwell House Hotel were a difficult and stressful time for all of us, especially for Mum, but being a big family really helped and of course life went on. We supported each other.

Another year rolled by and around this time, I left school and landed my first job. I think I was paid eighteen pounds and a few shillings a week. Not a bad wage really considering I was not the cleverest, and better than being in a shoe factory all day. However, boredom soon set in, and I wanted more than this. Richard steered me towards the military when he came on leave, and pretty soon I decided I would like to give it a go. I had not ventured far from home, as back in the eighties it wasn't as easy as today. But a big change was coming for sure.

The most important and rewarding time of my life came in 1974, when I had just turned sixteen years of age and was about to leave school. I got a decent job as an apprentice welder at a place on the A6 towards Kettering, but after a while I was bored, so decided to join the Army. What could be hard about that? See the world, meet people and take in some of the sights. I couldn't wait.

CHAPTER 2

You're in the Army now

My brother Richard was already in the Army, and he was always bigging it up, so off I went to the careers office in Kettering to see if I could do the same. My memories of this are a little sketchy, but they were nice guys and they sent me for selection to Leicester. I spent a couple of days there and the upshot was that I was accepted. Whoopee! I was off to a flyer.

My brother had been in the Army a while. He started as a cook in the ACC and then later in the RCT, and for all the doubters, he did his time on active service. He gave me valuable advice and helped me to draw up my list of options as follows: 1 ACC (Army Cadet Corps), 2 RCT (Royal Corps of Transport), 3 Infantry.

The letter finally arrived to tell me that I had passed. It was the Infantry for me. I was excited and worried at the same time. I decided I needed to get myself fit and prepare a little, as I had no idea about anything military apart from what Richard had told me. Fitness was never a problem for me, as I will explain later in the book. I had my hair cut short and read a little from the paperwork they give you. My attitude was that I would give it time and see how things progressed.

I remember that as I was walking home from work one Thursday I decided to go to the Army careers office. I really cannot remember much about the selection except that it was a couple of days away at Leicester. Of course, the army want you to join, so it was all positive and easy-going. I just had to do a couple of tests like basic mathematics and questionnaires. All of the staff were very helpful, especially In the early days, and everyone mixed in and chatted about which branch of the Army they would like to join. At the time I thought that being a guardsman would be pretty cool, and guarding

Buckingham Palace seemed to appeal, but apparently I was too short! On the other hand, patrolling in the jungle sounded good. I returned home excited and hoped I would be accepted.

At last the letter arrived, and I'd made it! I couldn't wait to get started. I had to report to IJLB (Infantry Junior Leaders' Battalion), Sir John Moore Barracks in Shorncliffe, Folkestone. I think a travel warrant came in with the letter, the first of many. This was around early September 1975, but I forget the exact dates now. I was excited, nervous and full of hope.

So, I caught the train to Folkestone and was pleased to see that a couple of guys who had been in Leicester were on the train, as there were quite a few joining that day. It was mostly nervous chat. I made a friend called Scratch, Mark being his real name, from Northampton. We got on well and agreed that we would stick together once we arrived. We went through the whole thing pretty much unscathed together.

After the Second World War the camp was known as the Sir John Moore Barracks, and from 1967 it was home to the Junior Infantryman's Battalion (JIB) and later, the Infantry Junior Leaders' Battalion (IJLB) until the dissolution of junior soldier recruitment in 1991. The Barracks were then used by regular infantry battalions. When the Light Infantry moved out in October 1986 the name was retained.

What a shock to the system! Firstly, we were given forms to fill in, then we had to report to get our equipment and uniform. Before we went in, they gave us our Army numbers. Mine began with 2438, but I didn't even have time to write it down. By the time we all had our gear and bed space sorted it was back outside to learn how to form three ranks. Then we were off for a haircut, though mine was short enough, I thought. Wrong! A short back and sides soon followed.

We were mesmerised by the shouting, the calling of names and numbers and wondered what had hit us, but we all worked together and helped each other with uniforms, as some of the guys had been cadets before joining. The staff taught us everything from bed blocks to ironing a shirt, and how your locker should look with all your uniform folded away nine by nine in its place, how to shape your beret and present yourself, how to address the staff. From this moment on we would 'double' everywhere – that means run. This had to be in the precise and military way, as was almost all movement around camp.

Learning how to march, or rather drill, being the correct military wording, was an eye opener, and there's more to it than meets the eye. But when carried out correctly it looks fantastic and I don't believe that any other army in the world could come anywhere close to the way we do it. It was all done by numbers and perfect timing, and every movement had to be precise. The drill instructors were immaculate, with not a hair out of place. We had to be exact, and believe me it takes plenty of time and so much practice to get to a presentable level, that is without a weapon to carry. Drill lessons were hard and repetitive until you got it right. But once it is right there is no better sight than an infantry platoon presenting arms to the shoulder, one of the best drill movements in the book, if not the best. The sight of a platoon or company marching on a full parade all in perfect unison is great stuff.

The training was hard and you had to learn real fast. If someone was struggling then we all helped out one way or another, especially with the fitness. I thought I had trained enough in my short time before joining up – wrong! It was really demanding, and for a little skinny kid like me, even harder, but there was always someone worse off. The guys who were carrying a little extra weight suffered, and in the main those who suffered most did not make the grade. My way of thinking was that I did not want to end up like those guys, shouting and being screamed at and almost being dragged up the hills by the instructors, no sir not me. I was going to keep going no matter what! I would use their failure as a reason to keep up.

The trick is to pace yourself and overcome the pain, simple as that. This not only applied in training but also carried over to battalion life in general, because it could still get hard at times.

On the train down to Folkestone when on leave one time, I thought it would be cool to look out of the window from the train. The next day on the drill square I had a cold in my eyes and could hardly look up. My eyes were streaming with tears and the drill instructor was right in my face screaming 'What are you fucking crying for boy, I'm your mother now! Now get on the floor and give me twenty push ups or I will stick this pace stick up your arse and march you round like a fucking lollipop!' Trying to explain was useless, and the expletives they could rattle off were unbelievable. You never answered back, or worse would follow. Trying not to laugh, I duly carried out my twenty, and then he was on to the next guy.

The fitness regime never stopped, and pretty much every day we would do the 'Hospital Hill' run. This was a killer and caught out many of the undesirables for sure. My trick was to take notice of what was going on around me and just keep going however much it hurt, legs burning and chest pounding, I felt sorry for some of the lads who really tried but just couldn't run. Their time was up.

Our first night out on the training area soon came, and as far as I can remember it was quite tame compared with what was to come later in my career. We were in combat uniform, obviously, but we did carry all of our gear, webbing, backpacks, doss bags and all the other equipment the way they had taught us – I'm not sure if had been issued weapons at this time. Well it was a bit of a jolly and quite relaxed. We were taught how to construct a 'basha' or bivouac, a small one-man tent if you like, just enough to get you and your gear in, about two feet off the ground and fixed between trees with bungee ties or rope. Then you had to camouflage it.

Off we all went, and when we had finished the staff came around and checked how we had done.

They told us to gather round a large fire, and we all had a beer and a singsong. This was where we learnt a few of the old Army songs that generally got belted out when we were pissed or in good spirits. My fellow Pompadours out there will know what I mean.

At about three o' clock in the morning when the rain was bucketing down, all was good. There were not too many leaks, just a damp patch here and there, but at about this time the staff paid us all a visit and I am sure they cut all the ropes to everyone's bashas and we were drenched. They woke us all up shouting how bad we were and told us our efforts were crap and we all had to make them again.

By the time all this had been done a few times and about one hour of sleep later, it was almost daylight. We had breakfast and doubled down the track to meet the four-tonners to take us back to camp. All of us were totally knackered and we couldn't wait to get on the trucks, but then the message came through that the trucks had broken down and we had to 'tab it' (TAB stands for Tactical Approach to Battle) back to camp. This was a ten-mile hike with all our gear, the first of many. It was all to test us who could handle it and weed out the no hopers, and we lost quite a few that night. I kid you not, the pain when you have a webbing belt digging in to your shoulder and rubbing your skin off is not great. OK, fixed that, but now I had a blister on my little toe. Just forget it, there's no time to stop, got to keep plodding on, ignore the pain, grit your teeth and get on with it. I looked around the next morning and more than half the intake were gone! Shit, we were still here...

A basha is a waterproof canvas or plastic sheet with eyelets or loops along the outside edge. They can be used when camping, outdoors or in military situations to provide shelter, shade and camouflage. Most often they are supported with bungee cords or string attached to trees. Bashas should be lightweight enough to be quickly erected and camouflaged in a pattern suitable to their terrain. A low profile gives a small silhouette and advanced models may be infra-red reflective or IRR.

For the first eight weeks there was no respite, no weekend passes and no chance to put a foot outside the camp gates. I had so much to deal with as a sixteen-year-old and I was homesick for a few days, but I vowed I would never quit after having come this far.

Learning went on, and not just military either – we also did some schooling, ie Maths, English etc. But of course, it went on how to deal with orders, cold, hurting, tiredness, kit inspections, bed blocks, drill, weapons training (we couldn't wait for that one), military etiquette, military history... there was so much to take in, and every day was a different challenge.

One of the most important things to learn for all of us was how to fire, strip and assemble, clean and accurately fire our weapons, which included GMPGs (general purpose machine guns), 66mm and 84mm anti-tank weapons, the 9mm Browning pistol, and of course hand grenades. To this end there were plenty of range days at Hyde ranges (I think that was the ranges we used), where we had to 'zero in' our personal weapons, so as to be more accurate when firing. This means basically firing a group of shots, inspecting the target to see where the rounds hit and adjusting sights as required, then doing it all again until you are shooting on target.

On a personal note, I really liked the range days and, of course, included was the fabulous, famous range stew. A four-tonner arrives and the cooks jump out, set up a line of food urns normally consisting of potato, stew, carrots, apple pie, custard or rice pudding, and we all line up with mess tins in hand and proceed along the line, filling mess tins at each urn – yummy. I recall one day I only had one mess tin, so along the line I had stew and potato, and just put the apple pie and custard on top. That day I had dessert before my main meal! And I cleaned the mess tin completely, because you get hungry on range days.

We all had to take our turn in the 'butts', which is down at the target end of the range, as well as lifting 'targets up' and 'targets down'. There was a bucket full of patches and sloppy paste to cover up the bullet holes ready for the next 'targets up'. It can be hard work in the butts and If I remember correctly it was a whistle blast for the up and down orders, so that all targets were raised and lowered in perfect unison. To fire these weapons was quite daunting at first, but practice makes perfect, and let us not pretend here, you are no good as an infantry soldier if you cannot hit a target at distance. I will always remember the kick in the shoulder the first time I fired the SLR (self-loading rifle). After that first one I made sure I did everything I had been taught and really got a good grip. That produced better results instantly. Once your technique is perfected the SLR is an awesome weapon. When you hit a target with the SLR it stays hit – that 7.62mm round can do plenty of damage.

Another personal favourite is the GPMG (general-purpose machine gun). I would say that, but then so would most other infantry soldiers. It's a fantastically accurate and very effective machine gun, and I think it is still used today.

The 66mm and 84mm are anti-tank weapons. The 66mm is a throw away once fired and is quite basic. You pull it open, line up the shot and fire, and it is pretty effective against soft-skinned vehicles. The 84mm Carl Gustav is better, same principle but this one is reloadable and a great asset to the section in case of tank threat. It can be fired by one man, but is most effective with a two-man team, one to load and one to fire. We fired both on a live firing range and it was great to get the experience.

Now to the hand grenade. Again there is a technique for throwing these things, but it works, and does the job for FIBUA (fighting in built-up areas) and in most clearance operations. Again, we did throw live grenades and added it to our experience.

Yes, we had some great days at the ranges. However, every now and again, especially in the early days, there would be another 'breakdown' in the transport, so we'd have to tab it back to camp again. This was done to help us get used to all the equipment we had to carry over a long distance, and improve stamina and fitness. To be honest, the more we did it the easier it was. The aim, as with most things, is that the more you practise the easier it becomes. I considered myself competent with the SLR and GPMG – I would not be making the battalion shooting team or sniper course, but I was not a bad shot.

After a few months, once the numbers had been reduced significantly, we felt we had earned more respect from the instructors. They were still hard, but they seemed happier with those of us who were left.

We were given tasks, both as a team or individually, and were given time as squad leader or 2IC, second in command. We learnt to be a team and to work for each other, which at the end of the day was what it was all about. If you were told to do something, you did it to the best of your ability.

Coming home on leave one time, I came from St

Pancras Station in London to get home to Kettering and was so knackered that I fell asleep on the train and woke up in Leicester. Luckily my Dad picked me up. I know my brother Richard had been in for some time, but Dad was proud of me I think. I had not seen my father in a number of years until that day, but without hesitation he instantly said, 'Stay put and I'll pick you up from the station'. We spoke once more after that at my brother David's house, quite some time after I had left the Army. Again dates are a little hazy, but it was around 2000, I think. He was in a bad way by then and had bone cancer, but he never complained. We recalled the aforementioned lift home and agreed that we should meet up one more time, but it wasn't meant to be. He always kept in contact with my sister Sue and only a short time after that conversation she told us he was gone. Shame we never met again. However, we did attend his funeral and we all said our farewells – he was still Dad, even after all that had happened.

CHAPTER 3

Passing out

So, life went on at IJLB. It was tough, especially in the early days, as I may have mentioned – repeat, refresh, re-learn and do it all again. As time moves on you are taught something new every day, and believe me there is so much to learn, even just the basics. Of course, as I was still only sixteen at the time, we still had to attend normal lessons. English, Maths and Science were the main subjects as I remember, although there may have been others. We also did History and of course Military, related to the units we were to join, recalling old battles and honours earned by the different regiments. To be honest, the mixture of lessons and military worked well, so our education also improved, as well as the soldiering side of things. We were getting fitter and stronger day by day, and as the year went by, we turned from boys to men for sure.

Anyway, we made it through the whole thing and when I was almost seventeen, we were ready. The passing-out parade was a parade and march past, and parents and family came to see us. A great day, and my Mum had a tear in her eye. She was so proud, and let me tell you, so was I. I would have liked my father to be there though.

My last word on IJLB was that I missed the last big hurrah, the end of year 'battle camp'. Unknown to me at the time, this was compulsory – I was told that before I could join the Regiment, I would have to complete the battle camp at the Queens Division Depot. However,, I had suspected appendicitis and was sent to Woolwich Military Hospital for two weeks while the others were on battle camp. After two weeks they said there was no need to have my appendix out, so I was to have a week's leave and report to the Depot afterwards.

Woolwich Military Hospital was massive, and

I think it took care of most of the Army. My time there was thankfully short. After several tests and plenty of prodding and poking about my stomach, it was deemed that no operation was needed at this time so after a couple of weeks, I was discharged with two weeks' leave and sent onward to the Depot at Bassingbourne.

We were in WMH for treatment for various ailments, and there was no need for rank. However, there is always one exception, and in this case, it was a big-mouthed Sergeant Major who made it known that he was in charge. As I remember he was not an infantry soldier, more like a rear echelon type.

Not for long. A few of us who had made friends during our short stay decided that we were not happy with this guy. There was a rota for tea making and each of us took our turn. We all agreed it was about time he learned his lesson, so we managed to obtain a sachet of laxative and during my turn one afternoon I added this to Big Mouth's afternoon cuppa. We were in fits of laughter, because about thirty seconds after he had drunk his tea he was up and running for the toilet like a man possessed. After this had happened two or three times, as I passed by his bed, I said to him, 'You really should be a little nicer to the lower ranks sir'. I think he understood then what had happened. I did not get a response, as within seconds he was off again heading for the loo! I never set eyes on him again. I was soon off home for a two-week holiday before heading out to the Depot, The Queens Division.

After all I had been through, I virtually had to start training again! It was only the last six weeks though. To cut a long story short I survived it, passed with flying colours and yet another passing-out parade later I was fit for the regular Army. This part is a real blank. I could not even tell you the names of the training platoon I was in, or give you any other names from that time.

The only event that stands out from my time at the Depot is the memory of a final room inspection. We were getting near to the end of training, so everything had to be immaculate. The bed space I was allocated had been vacated by a new recruit who had never made the grade. I had never really noticed. Usually squaddies have an assortment of pictures stuck on to their locker doors, typically of scantily clad or half naked girls, page three girls, pop idols or exotic cars stuck to their locker with Blu-tac or Sellotape, but not this guy.

So, with the inspecting group approaching – this includes usually the OC, CSM, Platoon Commander, training NCO and other hangers on of varying rank – we were called to attention. I stood to attention, with all of my kit laid out as per normal SOPs, with my now highly bulled best boots at the bottom, of the bed. As the Sergeant Major came nearer to my locker he started shouting 'what the fuck is that on your locker?' I did not have a clue what he meant, but on looking closer I saw that there was a picture of Hitler in uniform in some old picture shaking hands with some dignitary of some description.

The CSM went berserk and started swinging his pace stick around, too close to my head. I quickly grabbed the picture, ripped it off the locker and threw it down. It landed next to my best boots on the bed. Again, the CSM started to hit out with his pace stick and almost hit my boots, so again I grabbed for the offending picture and threw it over the locker, thus saving my boots from further attack.

After that the whole place went silent. On being questioned, I explained that having only been there a short time I had not noticed the offending picture and would most certainly have removed it if I had noticed. The Sergeant Major seemed happy with my explanation, he told me to make sure I found it and disposed of it as soon as possible. He then said my best boots looked very good! That was a close shave. I will never forget the look of anger on his face as he swung away with his pace stick, missing me by millimetres with every swing.

Once the inspection had finished and they had all left the barrack room, the whole place erupted in fits of laughter. None of us had ever seen anything like it on an inspection, before or since. I had to tell my fellow trainees that I honestly had not noticed the picture stuck on my locker, and maybe the outgoing guy had left it there on purpose.

The other stand-out memory from the Depot was the log runs. Ask any soldier who has taken part in one of these and he will tell you it Is hard training. Basically the 'log' is a telegraph pole. Each soldier takes his position along the pole according to height so everyone is bearing the weight of the log equally – if you didn't do that the short man in the middle would not even touch the log, never mind use any effort. Then you have to run with it over varying distances and also complete sit-ups or other exercises with the log. It is not very pleasant at all, and you certainly feel satisfaction if you can last the pace. Your timing needs to be perfect for switching the log from one shoulder to the other and you have to be in perfect unison when carrying out sit-ups, not to forget the obstacles you need to get over, and of course the deep mud-filled water holes you have to run through. But nonetheless it is a perfect way of training to be an infantry soldier. Hard, hell yes, but it is rewarding and gives you a great sense of achievement, and like most aspects of physical training, the more you do it, the easier it becomes.

So, I was pleased to get through this short period of training here to complete the basic training that had started a year before as a junior soldier in Sir John Moore barracks in Folkestone. There was no family at the final passing-out parade, as we had already done that at IJLB. Of course, the parade went well and then it was a matter of time before we all joined our different battalions. We were a mix of mainly Royal Anglians and Royal Regiment of Fusiliers as I recall.

I now had to wait for a flight out to Cyprus, which would be my first posting. While waiting I was posted to A company, not sure exactly where, as a Company runner. And so, entered into my life one Sgt Major M, a most excellent soldier and always immaculately turned out. I wanted to be this guy, because he was, and I mean no disrespect, the perfect military clockwork soldier, but whatever you do, do not wind him up! He had control of everything, and you could never get away with even a shirt button out of place. The memory of that bellowing voice shouting 'Runner!' still makes me shiver to this day. Never at any time did I miss one command of 'Runner' and I was always immaculate in my appearance. It was great preparation for the time ahead.

Every time he shouted 'Runner!' I had to bang my tabs in and be immaculate. One day he almost screamed it. I duly doubled in and banged to attention - 'Sir!' He said, 'Run to the NAAFI and get me one tube of fucking toothpaste and one tin of polish, it's a fucking emergency!'

'Yes, sir' I replied, then right turned, banged my right foot in hard, and marched off. But once out of the office it suddenly dawned on me that I had no money on me. Shit! I would have to go and ask him for some. After a couple of minutes, I plucked up the courage, fearing the worst, and knocked on his office door. 'Enter!' I banged my tabs in again and he bellowed 'Are you still here? Here's the fucking money soldier!' He slammed a note on the desk, one more deep breath and said, 'all things considered, shit for brains, you will be an asset to your regiment, now get out of my office before I change my mind!' I was gone, and as proud as hell!

My last word on this soldier was that one morning he ordered me to bring him a tea to his room at 0600hrs – some big parade or something. I barely slept, fearing that if I was late that would be my career over. When I arrived with the tea as ordered, to my surprise he answered the door in Army green 'grots' and vest, and to my amazement they were immaculately pressed, even starched I reckon, with creases in the perfect positions! Amazing.

I had the utmost respect for this Sergeant Major, as all things considered he was always fair and treated everyone the same. I had learned so much about discipline in that short space of time, as I used to watch and listen all the time to the way he dealt with certain situations, and the form of punishment always fitted the 'crime'. For example, if it was a dress code infringement it was normally a bollocking and being put on report, so the Section Commander could deal with it. If it was down to sloppiness in dress, then the offender had to put in more practice, or turn out and parading at different times in different uniforms. If he was reported for laziness or idleness, then extra drill would do the job. He was a stereotypical old school Sergeant Major, scary yet approachable – just.

I joined IJLB as a boy soldier, completed my final six weeks' exercise at the Depot Queens Division and was now joining the Battalion as a regular. I had finally made it. Well, almost...

CHAPTER 4

Cyprus and the UN

I have incorporated the United Nations tour alongside our tour in 1976 where we were a resident battalion, along with a return UN Tour in 1980, as I think the two go pretty much together. The first posting was for a resident battalion on the island – this was more of a presence on the island, and we trained just as a normal infantry battalion would do at home. The second however was as part of the United Nations peacekeeping force, where we wore the blue beret of the UN.

Here is the background as to why we were here

during the United Nations tour. Launched with relatively few troops, the Turkish landing had limited success at first, and resulted everywhere on the island in the occupation of Turkish-Cypriot enclaves by the Greek forces. On 23 July 1974, after securing a more or less satisfactory bridgehead, the Turkish forces agreed to a ceasefire. The same day a civilian government under Prime Minister Konstantinos Karamanlis took office in Athens, the day the Sampson coup collapsed. Glafcos Clerides became the Acting President in the continuing absence of Makarios.

Two days later, formal peace talks were convened in Geneva between Greece, Turkey and Britain. Over the course of the following five days, Turkey agreed to halt its advance on the condition that it would remain on the island until a political settlement was reached between the two sides. Meanwhile, Turkish troops did not refrain from extending their positions, as more Turkish-Cypriot enclaves were occupied by Greek forces. A new ceasefire line was agreed. On 30 July the powers agreed that the withdrawal of Turkish troops from the island should be linked to a 'just and lasting settlement acceptable to all parties concerned'. The declaration also spoke of 'two autonomous administrations – that of the Greek Cypriot community and that of the Turkish Cypriot community.

On 8 August another round of discussions was held in Geneva, Switzerland. Unlike before, this time the talks involved both the Greek and Turkish Cypriots. During the discussions the Turkish Cypriots, supported by Turkey, insisted on some form of geographical separation between the two communities. Makarios refused to accept the demand, insisting that Cyprus must remain a unitary state. Despite efforts to break the deadlock, the two sides refused to budge. On 14 August, Turkey demanded from Clerides acceptance of a proposal for a federal state, in which the Turkish Cypriot community (which at that time, comprised about 18% of the population and owned about 10% of the land) would have received 34% of the island. Clerides asked for 36 to 48 hours to consult with the Cypriot and Greek governments, but Turkey refused to grant any consultation time, effectively ending the talks. Within hours, Turkey had resumed its second offensive. By the time a new, and permanent, ceasefire was called 36 per cent of the island was under the control of the Turkish military. The partition was marked by the United Nations Buffer Zone in Cyprus or 'green line' running east to west across the island.'

The UK was having a heatwave, and we had one of our own in Cyprus – I remember stepping off from the VC10 and the heat just hitting me. So here I was on my first posting from Junior Leader to Regular Soldier, and I was ready. I would be hard pushed to even consider having a holiday in a place like this. It must have been thirty degrees. But what a beautiful place. More about the island later.

Shortly after this I was on my way to Cyprus to join the Battalion. I think I arrived in lightweight combats with all kit, Army suitcase and kitbag. I was dropped off at the guardroom, by bus I think – I'm not sure of this now, or how many of us there were.

So here I was, just finished training, ready to go, finely tuned and very fit, ripped I guess they would say now, and ready for anything. I went into the guardroom and banged my tabs in to the Guard Commander, Corporal 'Monty' B. I just marched in and stated 'Corporal, I am 2438...', but he interrupted with 'OK, enough of that, I am Monty, OK?'

'Yes, Corporal,' I replied, keen to show my

discipline, but he interrupted again. 'Look I am Monty, you don't have to keep calling me Corporal, your training has finished now. You have been assigned to One Platoon, their block is over there.' He pointed in the general direction. 'You need to report there asap.' I replied, 'OK Monty,' and he shouted back 'That's Corporal to you, sprog!'

A complete brain freeze. What the fuck was happening? Oh well, it looked as if I was going to have to get the hang of it somehow, but it was very hard to understand after the past year. Anyway, I learnt as time went on. It is difficult for civvies to understand – you always respect rank, but you also learn that there is a time and a place for it. It took me some time to work it out, if I ever really did. But a big thank you to Monty, as he was also my first platoon sergeant. Without his guidance and that of the rest of the Platoon, I probably wouldn't have lasted too long. Even now, despite playing a few different roles within the Battalion, these guys are the ones I cherish most, as this is where it all began. And let me tell you this, these men taught me so much, and not once did I feel threatened, bullied or in any way get mistreated. This is the Army, for God's sake, get on with it! Learning the hard way is possibly the best way to learn, because that way you never make the same mistake twice, and I had learned that lesson well.

On one occasion, I remember area cleaning outside the block area with the rest of the platoon when word came that an RP (Regimental Policeman) was asking for me at the road next to our accommodation block. Oh shit, what had I got up to? I was worried, so I doubled up to the road and there stood this RP staring at me from under his peaked cap. 'Are you Smith 37?' he asked. I replied, 'Yes staff'. He then shouted, 'You are in trouble soldier!' then with a grin he said, it's me, Danny from Rothwell, you prat!'

I just hadn't recognised him. I just could not put a name to the face – to be honest, he knew my brother better. Anyway, later he told me he had borrowed the RP's armband to wind me up. We went to the 'choggy [coffee] shop' for a coffee and egg banjo "roll" I think. I still owe him for that one. Danny now owns his own successful pest control business in Desborough and he's a great guy and a great ex-Pompadour. He was just slightly before my time. I think I am right in saying that he left shortly after our little meeting.

Whilst serving I still loved my sport, and I enjoyed football and made it into the Company team. I got a runner-up medal for I think getting into the semi-finals of the Army Cup. I came on as a substitute and played left wing. I remember making a couple of crosses, but alas we lost that one. I also believe it was broadcast on BFPO Radio, and it would be amazing if a recording of that game turned up somewhere. We had some great players and me being relatively new to the Battalion, the team looked after me well. Yes, they were great days, with great people – there is nothing that compares with the comradeship in the Army. We would all drink and socialise together and we would live and die together if we had to.

We also trained of course. Memory fades now, but I can recall carrying out weapon training and cleaning. The odd drill lesson was thrown in for good measure, as you never knew when the next big parade would come along, so we just covered all aspects on a daily basis, patrol techniques and section attacks, mostly carried out on the training area, but also there was plenty of room on camp to carry out the basics, such as weapon training and cleaning. In fact, I remember one of my first and most important jobs was being sent to the 'choggy' shop for the whole section and ordering and bringing back egg banjos and teas and such. I did as CPLM instructed, which was do as your told, keep your mouth shut and listen.

I cannot remember the reason I messed up one time, but we arrived for some sort of training one day, luckily quite close to camp, and I had forgotten to collect a piece of equipment. Well straight away I admitted my mistake, otherwise the whole Platoon would suffer and that is not correct. Anyway, as I recall I had the choice of a smack in the mouth or a 252, which is a formal charge in the military and a blemish on my so far good standing, so I took the hit, which was not that bad, think he held back. And I did have the choice. I found later that a charge against you is a definite pain in the backside. I deserved it, as in a real situation there are no second chances. But our Battalion routine went on, and in the military, you move on. We had plenty of free time for sunbathing and general rest and recuperation.

The island was a beautiful place, and for me, hardly ever having set foot outside the UK –
the furthest I had been was to Belgium on a school football outing – it was an amazing experience. So, to be there was surreal, and I often had to pinch myself.

The scenery was amazing. I will always remember the smell of the orange groves when we were on exercise. There was always an 'orange fight' whilst we were out and about, and some of the oranges were the size of footballs. If you got hit, you felt it. But of course, the oranges were a great source of energy and drink when on exercise, and refreshment when playing sport or on a run.

We were based in Limassol, which was quite a small town back in 1976 but has since grown somewhat. I remember visiting some ancient ruins there, Kourion I think it is called. There are plenty of ruins to visit all over the island, as well as Aphrodite's birthplace. There was an amphitheatre nearby and of course plenty of tavernas to drop into for a beer. We used to use the Amathus Beach Hotel, which was still being built when we were there and is now a five-star hotel I believe.

I will always remember my best friend at the time, 'Scratch', and me heading for the Amathus hotel one night, aiming to chat up the Swedish ladies who used to holiday there. We never quite made it, as the place was not busy enough because we had arrived too early for the nightclub to get into full swing, so we decided to try a couple of shots. Bad idea! I know Scratch started at one end of the bar and had a shot from every bottle there, and there must have been twenty different drinks. I believe it is called a Molotov Cocktail. I carried him back that night.

Most squaddies, no matter which country they are in, will take in the local culture and visit historical sites and other such places of interest. It is not always drinking time! We enjoyed and made the most of the island when we had time off. Sometimes though, things went a little too far. One such event was when a few of our guys hired a speedboat from Limassol Marina. Unfortunately, and no names here, they had all had a little too much drink and they got lost. Without a care, having had a few more beers, they just aimed the speedboat for dry land, right around the tip at Aya Napa and somehow landed in Famagusta on the Turkish-held side of the island. This was about a 60-kilometre trip, and it caused an international incident at the time as the governments on both sides had to sort it out, and it made the main news in the UK including Sky News. they were accused of being spies or even being sent by the British Army to 'recce' positions, when in reality it was just a couple of drunken soldiers let loose without a map. Finally, the whole incident was played down, and all sides saw the funny side. Those guys took a while to get over that one!

Workwise, life went on and I must admit, for my first posting, it was the perfect start. The guys in the platoon really helped me along. and I will take this opportunity to thank them all now. You see, in the Army you have people leaving and new recruits coming in on a constant basis, and you all have to stick together to make it work. There was no bullying in our day, we would just show the new guys how it worked, and it did. The change from junior soldier to a fully-fledged member of an operational battalion is a rewarding experience. It takes time, but you have plenty of time to learn.

So back to the routine again. Exact details are a little rusty now. We patrolled the border or peace line (buffer zone) regularly and carried out normal military duties, but we did have quite a bit of free time too, on a daily basis, as after 12 noon it was too hot to work.

I enrolled on a parachute course at Pergamos. I seem to recall the whole course being run by our very own Corporal Mick B, and I only paid 10 Cypriot pounds per jump. It was a fantastic experience and a real buzz to jump from a perfectly good aircraft, a Cessna 172 if I remember correctly. As always, we had to endure a couple of weeks' ground training (boring), but it had to be done, and thankfully it was done right. Our instructor, Corporal Mick B, was a top parachutist too.

When it came to the packing of parachutes, we were a little fed up until they said we would be jumping with the ones we packed the next day – everyone scrambled them back and double, no triple checked them! It was too windy for novice parachute jumps, so I went to the pool and tried to better myself by learning to swim (river crossings are quite daunting if you can't swim). It did help, but I still swim like a brick now. This lasted for only a few days until the wind had reduced so we could be cleared to jump.

Anyway, along came the day for our first jump. You had to climb out on to the step above the wheel and hold on to the cross member for the wing and dangle your leg. When the instructor tapped you, you pushed out and back and adopted the freefall position. WOW! The landing soon came upon you, and my god all you could do was steer these parachutes left or right. I found myself heading towards the orange groves, and I really did not want to end up dangling from an orange tree! Thankfully, I floated over them. The impact when you hit the ground is harsh, but if you land as you were taught, it all comes together nicely. It was a great feeling and I was amazed when afterwards Cpl Baxter said I was shit, arms all over the place. To be honest on that first one you really don't know what to expect, but it got better after that and by the tenth jump I was ready for dummy pulls, that is still on a static line but you go through the process of pulling the rip cord and it should be in your hand when you hit the deck. I would recommend anyone to try it, as it is exhilarating.

One morning the old caravan or shack we used to have a brew in and wait for the next jump was burnt to the ground. Because I was a cigarette smoker the finger was pointed at me, but I swear to this day, Cpl B, I am not guilty.

I also had my welcome, or should I say induction, into the battalion there, but the details will remain private. Suffice it to say it was not a very nice thing, but hey, when you're in you're in, and if you can't handle it you really shouldn't be there in the first place. But this would definitely not be classed as bullying.

Yes, 1978 was a busy year for us in Cyprus. Operationally we were scattered all over the island: Troodos about 6,000 feet up in the clouds, Agios Nikolaos near Famagusta, and our own camp at Episkopi. Training also took us to Pyla Ranges, near Larnaca Bay, and as far north as Akamas, a forgotten peninsula not that far from Turkey.

I remember that as part of our training in '77, we carried out an inter-platoon battle test in the form of a competition. It was in July if I recall correctly, and one of the hottest Julys on record. We concentrated on shooting and other basic skills. The test itself was an inspection, after which we were moved by vehicles, then ambushed, and then we had a TAB (tactical advance to battle), a forced march of 11 kilometres carrying all of our equipment, which weighed in at a hefty 60-80lbs, in 100-degree heat! We guzzled water every step of the way. This was swiftly followed by us setting our own ambush and finally we 'tabbed' another four miles, this time a 'speed march' to the end of the exercise on the ranges at Akrotiri. I am at a loss as to where we ended up, but I think Recce Platoon won it. It was hard and gruelling, but we loved it. Every platoon took part and I believe there were a couple of high-profile dignitaries attending, and they were mightily impressed.

Being a 'sprog' or newcomer to the battalion, I got my head down and got on with it, and with great mates and teamwork we all made it through. They were great memories that will never fade. However, I'm sure the officer in charge who led us on the tab took us through the same village two or three times, and I remember saying to one of the lads 'we have been here before fucking twice already.' He agreed, but we kept on with the tab. Historically, Officers are never very good with maps. But fancy tabbing 10 miles in 35 degrees heat!

On the 11th January we visited Malta on Operation Turnabout. We were housed at Ghajn Tuffieha Barracks north of Golden Bay via RAF Luqa. Here we trained to practise our shooting skills and carry out minor exercises at Hal Far airfield. We were assisted by 41 Commando and taught familiarisation in Gemini assault boats and Gazelle helicopters. We were also taught rock climbing and survival training with 41 Commando.

I recall that on our R and R time in Malta we visited a church, I think in Valletta. The capital and the Mosta Dome Church had been bombed during the Second World War. However, in this particular church the bomb had not exploded, and it was still in the exact spot it had dropped into, so the church was now a major tourist attraction. I must say it was a beautiful church, and I remember especially the pattern of squares on the ceiling. The roof was a massive dome shape. So, it was pleasing that the bomb never exploded as it would have ruined a beautiful building.

It was a long hot summer for sure, but at least for our hard work we were rewarded with nights out in historic Valletta and medieval Rabat. Two weeks of hard training was soon over with plenty learnt, and we were wiser men when we returned to Cyprus a couple of weeks later.

On one crazy night out after a hard day's training we all decided that we would have a couple of drinks in the NAAFI, then head into town for one of the night clubs. What could possibly go wrong?

There were about 10 or 12 of us and we were having a great night. After the NAAFI we had a few in the local pubs before going to the night club. We arrived at the Famous Kings Disco a little too early and found the place almost empty. Anyway, we sank a few more beers and all of a sudden, the place started to fill. We squaddies always liked to chat up the locals and keep friendly with them, but it all got out of hand when some local guy tried to sit on Steve N's knee. After a couple of warnings, the guy was duly clobbered by Steve, and with that all hell broke loose. The local Cypriots just came from nowhere and one hell of a fight ensued. We gave some out and received a few knocks ourselves, but we managed to escape down the stairs to the exit – why was I the last one?

Anyway, we ran into the street and the punch-up continued there. By now we were vastly outnumbered. I tripped on the kerb and was immediately surrounded and being kicked all over. I protected myself as best I could and covered my head with my arms. At that moment the police arrived, and the locals backed off. When I looked up from the floor all I could see was these mates of mine waving and cheering and saying, 'Come on Smudge, you're doing great!' But they were about a hundred yards away on the other side of the street! Fortunately, I escaped with only bumps and bruises. What a mess.

We were all arrested by the local police and shoved in to Land Rovers to be taken down to the station. The police followed on behind so there were two Land Rovers and two police cars, Volkswagen Beetles I remember.

One of my mates, Kev B, said to me that he was already in trouble and the RSM had warned him that if he made one more slip-up he would be locked up. As we slowed to take a corner in the road, he jumped, rolled onto the ground with a parachute roll and ran. The convoy stopped and the police suddenly pulled out their pistols and started waving them around. But they soon gave up looking for Kev and followed us the rest of the way in a car behind with pistols pointing at us.

Once we arrived at the cells in the local police station, the Duty Guard Commander came from camp and we all had to make statements. By this time, it was almost daylight. We marched from the Guardroom to the RSM's office still covered in blood, with clothing ripped and black eyes and cuts to almost every one of us. Most of the rest of the battalion were just awake and heading for breakfast, so all eyes were upon us.

The RSM was not pleased. We did explain that the locals had been calling the British Army and in particular our regiment a bad name, but he kept repeating the question 'Who was the one that got away?' We said we were so drunk that we honestly could not remember. To our amazement he let us all off with a warning, and Kev lived to fight another day, if you will excuse the pun.

Yes, in general we all behaved outside camp, but by the same token we will not let anyone out-fight us either!

Another grand occasion in Cyprus was of course the Queen's Silver Jubilee. As I mentioned earlier, you never know when there is a big parade just around the corner, so drill practice is always useful. We had to get the rust out of us, as we had not drilled for some time, and we had to remember the moves, with weapons. Of course, the Silver Jubilee parade came along, and it was practice drill, more drill, and then some more drill. The lightweight Number 2 dress really helped in that heat. I don't think these looked as good as the Number 2 dress we wore back in the UK, but it was extremely comfortable in the heat of the day there.

The parade was held on the 3rd June at Happy Valley, and the commander of the parade, Lt Col D, paid tribute to Her Majesty with a 21-gun salute from HMS *Mohawk*, which was anchored in the bay. I will never forget the noise from those guns as it echoed around the valley. Then we gave our own 'Feu de Joie', a rifle salute with each soldier along the ranks firing in turn to give a continuous rat-tat-tat effect. There was also a Royal Air Force fly-by with a Nimrod, escorted by three Canberras, and helicopters. This was followed by the usual march past taken by the Commander British Forces Cyprus, the Air Vice-Marshall.

We were thankful of the lightweight No. 2 Dress in the heat of the day, but even so we were still dripping with sweat. It was a great parade to celebrate the Queen on her 25th anniversary.

I really enjoyed both my tours in Cyprus and would like to get back there one last time. It was a first look at a foreign country for me and I think most Pompadours would agree it was a great tour. It was a fantastic place for my first posting overseas. In a short space of time I had learnt to be a pretty good rifleman and settled in to the battalion, and I was pleased with the way it was all going.

On the grapevine the word was that our next posting would be Northern Ireland – not yet, surely? But by the time the Cyprus posting came to an end with a move to Bulford, we knew that yes, the next posting was to be to Northern Ireland.

CHAPTER 5

Into the Troubles

We were posted to Bulford/Tidworth to undergo our NI Training in 1978. I do not remember much about the training except that there was a mock town where we honed our patrol techniques and were prepared for and practised different scenarios. This is FIBUA or fighting in built up areas, ie coming under fire, IEDs, booby traps and riot situations. Most people tend to look inwards or are drawn towards a distraction, but you really need to cover your arc of fire and be constantly observing doors, windows and the people around you. We also practised riot control, which looks messy, but with training you can manipulate the rioters in a direction they do not wish to go, thus easing the tension away from the main trouble spot. At least we would try to accomplish that, but in reality it is very different. There were endless foot patrols around the mocked-up streets, which I have to say was realistic. We were dealing with different scenarios, from dealing with booby trap devices to trying to arrest a known suspect. Of course, sometimes we would be in vehicles (Land Rovers) and we also practised patrolling in them, and how to operate a vehicle checkpoint, which is a regular occurrence on the streets when you maybe need to cut off an escape by a known terrorist. As always, we practised our shooting on an indoor range using the Heckler & Koch weapon with .22 rounds. It was not bad for the seventies; different films were played and sometimes you hit the good guy (collateral damage). Again though, practice makes perfect.

All in all, the training went well and by the time we were due to head to Belfast, we were ready.

We were posted to Palace Barracks just outside of Belfast, in a town called Hollywood. For sure this was the real deal, and we knew it was time to earn our pay. Before the posting we were allowed on leave to visit family, and I remember Mum saying that I wasn't allowed to go, and I replied, 'Try telling that to the Sergeant Major'. It was a worrying time for all concerned at the time, and it seemed as if it would just rumble on for years, as indeed it did. There were plenty of shootings and bombings on a daily basis but unlike now, they were never reported in the press or on TV.

There must have been literally thousands of mums up and down the country all saying the same as mine, that they didn't want their sons to go to Ulster. Every mother knew that there was a real chance that her son might not be coming home. I wrote and telephoned regularly from the old phone box to keep her from worrying too much. We would also write letters home when possible, just to let the family know we were fine, and it was all great, so not to worry, we would be home in no time at all. We also said that it was really easy, and we were not on the street much, which of course was not true, but it put my mum's mind at ease, I think.

The posting was for one and a half years. Normally at that time units were sent over to the Province for four-month tours of duty, although they stayed in one place for the duration. In our case it was into Ballymurphy for two or three of weeks at a time and then R and R back at Palace Barracks. This was to be the routine.

Anyway, as an eighteen-year-old I was shitting bricks, because it is not nice to be in fear for your life almost every day. No, it wasn't Afghanistan or Iraq, but it was the same sort of fear, and at least in those conflicts they had the chance to return fire. On every patrol you had to be on the ball. We just did as we had practised – keep your eyes open and be ready for anything. Can you imagine walking through the streets of an estate in your home town and a sniper opening up on you, or a lamp post blowing up as you walk past it? Or two or three masked gunmen jumping out of an alleyway to take a pot shot at you?

We had the art of patrolling nailed after a while and it becomes second nature after a couple of times on the street, although being the tail-end Charlie takes some practice. That means patrolling backwards, and you do rely on your opposite number to make you aware of lamp posts etc. You really cannot relax for a second, or shit happens, and you are not ready. And then you're dead.

When you stop on patrol, you do not stay in the

same place for too long – you do the unexpected, ie dart across the road and back to a different position. If you do, crouch for a while and 'balloon' – that is, move your body and head constantly so a sniper can't hold you in his sights long enough to get a shot off. All of this takes communication with other members of your 'brick' (four-man unit), and the truth is you trust these guys with your life and vice versa.

Rioting is also a scary situation, and it usually starts from nothing. For instance, while you are checking someone, things get a little heated, and then the dustbin lids will start banging, which is a call to bring out the other locals, and it soon escalates. Before you know it, a large crowd has gathered, and the younger ones start pelting you with stones and bottles. Of course, some of these were planned to lure your patrol into an ambush, when they would open fire on you.

On one occasion we were patrolling the 'Murph' and outside the shops, I think on Kelly's Corner, when our commander spotted a known and wanted IRA member. We tried the softly-softly approach, but the bastard ran like a rabbit, so there was our brick and a street full of them chasing us chasing him. He hid in one of the terraced houses, so Bob Mac kicked the door in and we followed suit. They tried to hide him, but we found him cowering behind a cupboard, but then a woman with a child in a buggy stood in our way and blocked us getting to him. No chance – he wasn't getting away. We finally got him onto the street. We had already called for back-up, usually a couple of Land Rovers or a 'Pig' (light armoured vehicle) to pick him up. The street was packed, and we were getting lots of abuse. Fuck knows where they all came from, but it really was a big crowd. There were only four of us and fifty to seventy screaming civilians who wanted to kill us were getting closer by the minute, a scary place to be. Bob Mac said that if they not here soon, we going to have to let him go. No chance of that, we agreed. Then a pig arrived in the nick of time. We were expecting to be contacted (fired on) at any minute, but thankfully, it never came. The terrorist was arrested and taken and handed over to Springfield Road RUC station. One less to worry about.

We all piled into the Land Rovers and made good with our getaway. Another few minutes and all hell would have broken loose.

* * *

It has taken me a hell of a time to write this from the start, some two years ago as I write, but I have gained inspiration not only from the missus but also with the knowledge that with the events that I will now describe, I am really privileged to still be around.

It is Wednesday the 5th of October. I have been hospital today as my back is hurting bad with severe pain at the base of my spine. It has been gradually worsening as I get older. I was diagnosed around 1990 as having a hemi-vertebra, a curved spine, but I also have a crumbling mess at the base. Have an epidural or man up, I was just told. I will opt for the latter. Also, on this day I was reading a post on Facebook about John V, one of our own band of brothers. His funeral will be in Aldershot at the end of the month. I had only just got back in touch with John after 40 years and was so looking forward to seeing him again, but alas it was not meant to be. However, JV deserves a mention here, as not only was he a great Pompadour but also a true gentleman. I recall in the early days John issuing me with a travel warrant or two to come on leave. I am sure between him, Nigel H, Don H and Nigel B they kept the battalion going with reams of paperwork.

Anyway, it got me to thinking that my minor back problem pales into insignificance in comparison with other people's problems. At least I am still going, so RIP John and all other Pompadours who are no longer with us. Great guys one and all.

So, get on with it Smudge and stop whinging. Mind you I did know that backpack with the mortar barrel was too much for my skinny little legs. Now back to the memoirs.

* * *

Ulster was relentless, day in and day out. We were lucky that we had good old Palace Barracks to go to after one of our stints in the 'Murph' – the lads stationed there on four-month tours did not. Before my next story I must write about the day we lost one of our lads, not to the evils from outside the camp gates, but from within.

Of course, you keep training and keep fit, and you keep the mind active or you will lose your sanity. One day we were on the assault course with the twelve-foot log, or telegraph pole almost. There was a knack to being able to get over the assault course with one of these things. We had all done it in our basic training and it was good fitness training to carry that tradition on within the battalion. On this particular day though, it all went horribly wrong. We were tackling the twelve-foot wall towards the end of the course, and it was released too early and hit one of the guys on the other side, a lad called Paul 'Fossy' Foster. He took the full force of it and unfortunately died almost instantly. The paramedic was on the spot in seconds but unfortunately nothing could be done. He was a great guy and a great fellow Pompadour. Paul was remembered by a new assault course trophy, the Foster Trophy. He never had the chance to take on the IRA.

Back to the street once more and the daily grind continues. You wonder if you will make it through the day. You must keep moving, take cover every time you stop, and keep alert, all the time – think 'the bastards are not getting me, not today'. I guess some of the lads had lucky charms or such items to keep them alive. I asked God to keep me alive please, but after a while I realised it wasn't up to him, if there even was such a thing as God, it was down to me – to do as I was trained, think, look, listen and all will be good. Only another six or seven months to survive. Feel sorry for yourself when you RTB, not out here, and it will get you killed. You have a responsibility to your 'brick' – you need each other. We will survive. Let us get out there, let's do the job, and you keep repeating it over and over and over again.

We had been out here for some time, though dates escape me. Word was out that we were to cover an REME convoy on its way to bases in bad areas in the south of Ulster, Armagh, also known as 'bandit country'. So instead of the normal street patrols and FIBUA, we were going back to the nitty gritty that we all loved, camouflage and concealment, full equipment, camouflage cream, back to the sticks. It was great to get respite from the streets, and it came at exactly the right time, as we were all getting a little downhearted.

Bob Mac trained us hard for a couple of weeks, and we needed it, because if you switch off from it, it is easy to forget the basics. Everyone in the camp looked on amazed as we ran past with full kit, cam cream, 'tin lids', the whole works. On the last day of retraining we finished just outside the Plastic pub (oh the memories) and Bob Mac turned to as all and said 'you spunking lot are ready... last man inside buys the first round!'

We were deployed I think close to the South

Armagh border. The IRA patrolled like the British Army, only with AK47s, M16s, RPGs and balaclavas. Had we bumped into any on route they would have been screwed.

We finally reached our position late. We could just see the road the vehicles would use in the distance and started to dig in – not good as the ground there was rock solid, so we just dug in as best we could, just a couple of feet I recollect. We fortified the position as per SOPs (standard operating procedures) with trip flares and claymores and got sentries posted. I had done my stag (sentry for two hours) and then bedded down.

Me and Smudge nine zero shared our position. We camouflaged it as best we could and the whole unit settled down in perfect silence.

Then at about three-thirty hours, all hell broke loose. Trip flares went off and lit up the night sky, which they are supposed to do. I have never moved so fast in my life, or even for my life. We were both out of our doss bags with rifles cocked in firing position from fast asleep in about six seconds flat, hearts pounding. We covered our arc of fire, and I shit you not, if anything moved it would be chewing on a minimum of twenty 7.62mm rounds. The flares dimmed and then just the black sky and silence, then a few voices from the guys who investigated. 'Stand down' was the word. Apparently, a cow had set off the trip flare. Safety catch on. We were relieved but also on edge, as our position was compromised, however we had to stay put to cover the convoy. We did so with success. At daybreak we bugged out and patrolled back to the RV.

Anyway, Smudge 90 and I both reckon that seven to ten seconds from doss bag to firing position is shit hot! Another real-life experience but carried out by some of the best soldiers ever.

Well that was fantastic but short lived, so now back to the streets and back to the 'Murph', a complete shithole crawling with the rotten terrorist bastards.

On another occasion, we were doing our regular patrolling close to the time when internment was introduced, which meant that a person arrested could be held for 48 hours without being charged. This was 'celebrated' every year with bombs, hijackings, shooting practice and burning of vehicles in general. Basically, it was a free for all for the IRA, and of course they used it to entice any patrol into a danger zone where they would be ambushed or blown up.

We all needed to be on top of our game at that time – although we were always on edge, it was more prominent in this situation. We had just finished our patrol and were heading back into camp when shots were fired, and the rounds went no more than a foot or so over our heads. You never forget the 'crack' and 'thump' when it gets that close! A very distinctive sound, and we thought it was probably an AK47 or even an Armalite – an M16 rifle. One of the lads thought he had spotted the area where the shots came from.

Anyway, we were zig zagging into camp, but now we wanted to go back out and chase down the gunman, so with adrenaline rushing and wanting to catch the bastard we regrouped, reloaded and were just about to go back out when an officer from the battalion taking over said to Colour Sergeant Bob Mac, 'No don't bother Colour, let them calm down a little'. I think Bob Mac's reply was something like 'you are taking the piss sir!' However, an officer had given the order so we could not go. Disappointed would be a fucking understatement.

We certainly earned our pay out there, and I'm sure most would agree we enjoyed the challenge, but not being allowed to shoot back is a kick in the nether regions. It was very rare to get a shot at one of them, especially in the open. To lose one of your own and do nothing about it was also a sore point, especially when they singled out an unmarked escort – that was when we used to escort workers from hospitals using an unmarked vehicle, wearing civvies and carrying the Browning 9mm pistol for protection.

The IRA were not stupid and sometimes you stood out like a sore thumb. On one occasion, October 8th 1980, Paul W and L/CPL Nobby C were ambushed on the Falls Rd/Whiterock Rd junction. Five balaclava-clad gunmen jumped out as the vehicle was turning and fired directly into the car. Paul was murdered instantly, shot in the head, but the other guy returned fire and although hit I think four times he managed to run towards the camp. Once the sentries realised what was happening, they also returned fire. We all got a little more aggressive after hearing the news about this one, but we couldn't do shit about it. Thankfully, Malcolm made a full recovery, but Paul did not. RIP Paul, duty done, remembered always, especially on Remembrance Day.

On another occasion in Ireland, we were operating a vehicle checkpoint. This was where two Land Rovers blocked the road on opposite sides so as to form a 'slow area' where the vehicles had to pass through. Once stopped, the people in the vehicles were 'P checked', then the vehicle was searched and then moved along.

We had set up the VCP and my position was at the front of the second Land Rover. Suddenly a yellow Mk 3 Ford Cortina drove at us at some speed. It was obvious he was not going to stop, so we all dived for cover. Once I recovered, I adopted the kneeling firing position and controlled my breathing, then took aim into the back window of the Cortina... I was a hair's breadth from squeezing the trigger when my vision opened up and I could see people on the street. I thought for a millisecond and realised that if I hit the driver the car would swerve and run into a passer-by, or a stray round could ricochet and again hit someone nearby, so I decided not to open fire. Restraint and professionalism showed again.

Did the occupants realise how close they came to be shot? Are they still alive today? I will never know or care, but Lady Luck was certainly with them that day. They were using that vehicle as a weapon, to try and kill us, and these were people whom it is my duty to protect. There were other reports of this, and soldiers sometimes did open fire. The order came down from the higher echelons that we were no longer to open fire as too many 'joy riders' were getting shot or killed. What did they expect?

A similar thing happened in 1988 – it was all over the news. Two undercover corporals in an unmarked car drove into a funeral after taking a wrong turn and were dragged from the car, beaten and shot, and their battered bodies dumped later. Although I had left the Army by then, it made me physically sick. It is easy to say with hindsight, but if ever I was in that situation, I would have taken out twelve of the bastards and kept the last round for myself. There are 13 rounds in a Browning 9mm magazine.

That was the real deal, being scared for your life, shot at, spat on, trying to stop five thousand screaming people from rioting, people who would kill you in the blink of an eye. You were wondering every time you set out on patrol if it was your turn today. It's not surprising that a problem which affects plenty of military people today is post-traumatic stress disorder, which appears to be a recent discovery. I know of a few members of our own battalion who still suffer PTSD to this day, forty years after the event, no names required. To be honest I think we all have it, but we all deal with it in different ways

– mood swings, feeling depressed, worthless, angry, nightmares etc, and unfortunately some suffer to the point of suicide. Only if you have been there and done that will you know how it feels, and it must be a hard cross to bear. If you are one of those who suffer PTSD, keep strong and never give up!

This tour had seen the battalion drawn closer together, as we had to depend on each other for our lives. We built up stronger bonds between each unit, be it section, platoon or company. We worked hard in all weathers and difficult circumstances and came out of it with success. We all had self-discipline and respect, and we all had the honour of not letting down our mates, the battalion, the regiment and our country. Most of us came out the other side intact, but some were not so lucky. We lost a few great Pompadours in Ulster, and they will never be forgotten. Personally, I truly believe we did some good, in terrible situations. We were always professional and carried out any given task by the book and to the best of our ability.

Peace came to Northern Ireland in the 1990, and I rest my case.

You're not supposed to blow your own trumpet, but I was getting pretty good at this soldiering stuff by now, and I had been in a few years too, having mostly kept my head down and done as I was told. I was now into my fourth year and handling it well. With encouragement from mates and my Platoon Commander I was volunteered, no selected, to try the PNCO cadre. This is where you attain a little rank and earn a couple of extra shillings. A Lance Corporal is a section second in command and does hold quite a bit of responsibility, while a full corporal is the section commander, so I needed to learn what he knows and be able to take over the section if required, either in a live operation or peacetime. For instance, the section commander may be away for some time and hand the reins over to his Lance Corporal. A daunting prospect believe me. It's not so bad in peacetime if your dossing around camp, but in the field it's a very different ball game. However, I was ready for it and really wanted to show the knowledge I had accumulated.

As it happened the cadre was run by my Platoon Commander, C/Sgt Mac, one hell of a great leader and well respected, but I knew this was not going to be easy. To explain a little more, this is like going back to basic training. Obviously, we all had to take our turn as commander but also of course we were back to private soldiers so that everyone could be assessed.

This course included everything:

1. Weapons training, giving lessons on SLR/GPMG/Browning 9mm, a class of about twenty each time, so you need to know the subject. Question and answer sessions.

2. Drill/discipline. Controlling a squad of soldiers to get around in an orderly manner. Dress code, cleanliness, correctly turned out at all times.

3. Tactics. Patrol techniques, different types of patrol, crossing open ground, covering fire, camouflage and concealment, survival. How to give a set of orders for a mission, map reading. Controlling your section. Decision making. Flanking manoeuvres. Fire and manoeuvre. These are just a selected few.

4. Man management. Looking after your section, looking after your health, how to keep warm, sleep deprivation. Eating, energy, adapting. Buddy system. Break the boredom, staying switched on.

5. Military etiquette.

Anyway, the course was hard, as we all expected, especially the final exercise, but I came out the other side of it with a pass, and not just a pass – I actually was given first place! I was closely followed by my mate Ian C. We were sure it was close, and I honestly thought I had made top five. (No Ian, it was not because my Platoon Commander ran the course. I was just better.)

I must also mention the instructors. They pushed us really hard but were always on hand to assist, and without those guys we never would have made it. They helped us every step of the way and were always approachable, although they might say 'Fuck off Smudge, you should know that!' I may be a little rusty fellas, but Geordie C, Steve D, Phil P and Bob Mac, Course Commander, thanks to you all. Most of the names on the course I will not have known and definitely cannot remember now. Quite a few passed and not many failed. Sorry Ian, someone had to come second!

My final word on gaining my first 'stripe' is that it is really hard to get on the ladder but so easy to lose it and drop down a rung, so standards can never drop.

The immense pride I have for achieving this

lowly rank will stay with me for life. You fellow squaddies out there will understand, but the rest of you will just have to believe me. I cannot compare it to anything in Civvy Street. Nothing comes close. I suppose if you were promoted from a shop floor worker to supervisor it would come close, but you would never have the same level of responsibility as we did.

My final chapter on the Northern Ireland story rumbles on to this day, and not in a good way. To bring you up to date, recently there has been a spate of prosecutions against ex-soldiers who had served in Northern Ireland.

Now before I go on, to bring the peace in the province we had the so-called 'Good Friday agreement'. included in this agreement is a statement that ex-members of the terrorist organisation cannot be prosecuted for past offences – in fact not only that but most were given a 'get out of jail free card' which kept them immune from prosecution and indeed they were actually released from prison. Surely then it is wrong to then try and bring about prosecutions of soldiers in the same situation? It seems not. Now such prosecutions are ongoing, but surely it is about time that the very government that sent us there to serve and protect gave us the same immunity as the terrorists themselves.

This extract was discovered on Facebook recently. I apologise to the guy who wrote it for reproducing this as I did not get his name, but he puts the point across. Please read on:

Northern Ireland was a tragedy, a cock up, and it was brutal for all those involved. The civilian police could not cope with the situation, so the British Government sent in the troops, men who were trained to shoot and kill the enemy in event of war. They were sent in with little or no training of urban peacekeeping or acting as a civilian police force. We were tossed into this utter political mess and social bucket of shit with not a clue. The officers and NCOs had to make it up as they went along. A big learning curve for all, to say the least. Yes, the government came up with the 'Yellow Card' to cover their arse, but the soldiers on the ground had milliseconds to make life-saving, or indeed life-ending, decisions. Mistakes were obviously going to be made – after all the place was in a state of chaos and rule of law had broken down. We were facing an enemy that hid behind women and children, would booby trap lamp posts so that patrolling soldiers were blown up on passing, or cause a riot and draw the soldiers in before opening fire with petrol bombs and AK47s, who could shoot at you from any window or doorway in the whole estate and then just disappear. Do we return fire at the risk of a deflected round hitting a passer-by, or should we do as we did in almost every contact – hold back and try to follow up as best we could? Probably we'd find the spent cases, but the terrorist was long gone. They had no rules or yellow card to restrain them. The Army were tasked with taking control and defeating a hidden terrorist enemy on both sides, a very difficult and dangerous situation. Now is the time for the Government to put a stop to this. If there are to be no prosecutions of the terrorists with their get out of jail free card, then there should also be no more prosecutions of British soldiers.

When I awoke every morning to head out into the streets of the Ballymurphy, scared for my own life, I did not say 'right, I am going to kill somebody today'. We were doing our job, for fuck's sake. The government should put its hand in its pocket and pay compensation to all families, including the 'bad side' for those that lost loved ones, and then draw a line under the whole mess. They should say 'Yes, we put them there to do a job and they did it. Now let us move on'.

From a military perspective, we learned the hard way, but we have the skills and knowledge now to deal with such a situation if it was, God forbid, ever needed again. The blood of veterans that served in Northern Ireland is now the foundation of our modern strategies.

Well, we finally made it through, and I really could not wait to get back to England. At last we were off to Colchester and home.

Platoon 1976, when I had just joined. I'm in the centre

Drill lesson

Typical locker layout

Platoon soccer team

Training on the chopper with 41 Commando Royal Marines, Malta

needs caption

Silver jubilee

UN observation post on the buffer zone

Bashas in the woods

Inter-company boxing

Colchester ABC

Fighting a seven-foot guardsman

Receiving a runner-up medal, 1976

With 1 Platoon, A Coy., Cyprus 1976

Belize patrol

needs caption

Rideau camp, Belize

sunbathing at Rideau

Simmo making a brew, Belize

needs caption

NBC training

Ready go in my daily attire for NI.
The strap is for a riot gun

Time for a brew, NI style

Firing on the move

In veteran's dress

needs caption

with Roy Holohan

Discussing Roy's antics

Norwich reunion

Ethan on patrol

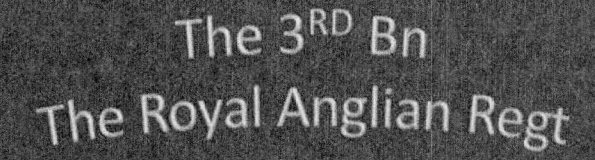

Pompadours

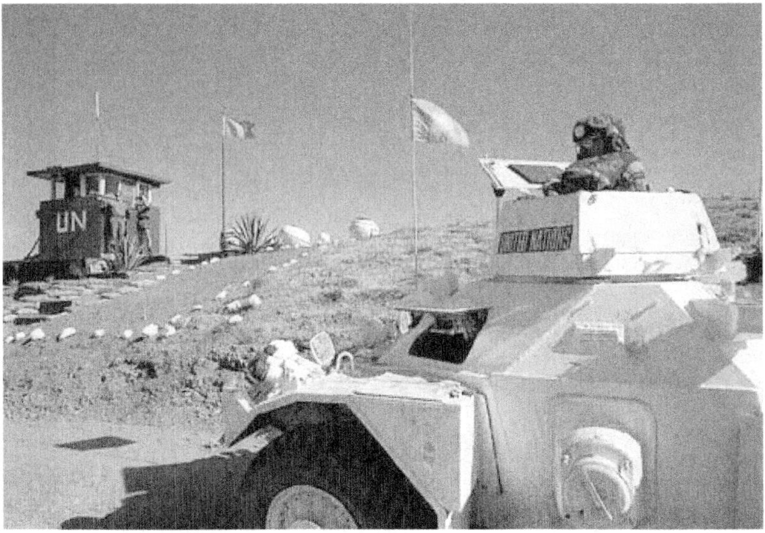
UN

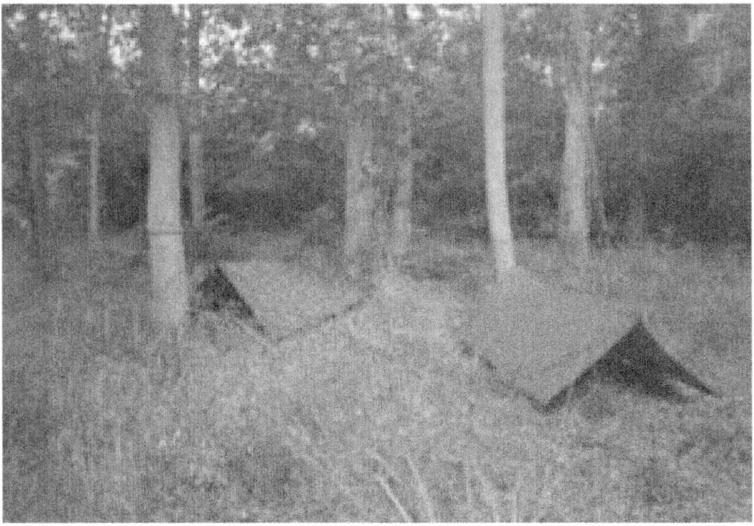

CHAPTER 6

Colchester, 1979-1984

Colchester was one of the biggest garrison towns in the country, if not the biggest, and a truly great place for our battalion at this point. We travelled to several different postings from here, and the dates I mention will only be a rough guide.

Colchester had everything a soldier could want for back in the eighties – pubs, clubs, the town for shopping, all the amenities you would need, snooker rooms, gymnasium, boxing ring for sparring, sports fields, and most of it was in the confines of the camp area. I was in married quarters in Colchester, had a nice flat a mile or so from our camp, which was Meeanee Barracks, close to the town centre. I do believe quite a few of the old Pompadours still live there to this day. Also, to me, back in the eighties, it was home, and I wished I had stayed there. I loved every minute of it, well almost all of it. Having said that, going back recently I could not live there now as it's too over-populated for me.

The first thing we had to contend with, at Bulford I believe, was the visit of the Queen Mother. This took weeks of marching practice and preparation of best dress and it seemed to go on forever. We were seasoned veterans now, so it did not take long for us to look immaculate on the day and let me tell you there is no finer sight than the British Army in full flow performing drill. One for the old sweats, from the present arms to the shoulder is the best drill movement ever. And when carried out correctly it looks fantastic.

Anyway, time rolled on and come the big day of the parade we were ready. It must have taken about ten minutes before the heavens opened and it started to rain. It just got heavier and heavier, until we were all drenched. Not one crease was left in our well-prepared and immaculate number two dress and our best boots were ruined.

We waited almost two hours for the Queen Mum to arrive and proceeded to drive along the front rank in a golf buggy-type vehicle. I can't remember if she got out. The trick to standing for so long in the same position is to slowly roll forward on the balls of your feet and tense your leg muscles. We also got away with a bit of chat, through gritted teeth. When you see the guys pass out at these parades, it is because they do not move enough to keep the blood circulating, and consequently down they go. Well we were drowned rats that day, for sure. A great piss up after though. Yes, nobody came up from home this time, but we did have a fantastic day. Colchester was a great posting for us at the time, and we had certainly earned it from the Ireland tour.

I'm not sure of the order but I think it was Belize next for us, out in the jungle, so that meant another set of skills for us to learn. I loved every minute of it. I just remember the humidity hitting you as soon as you stepped off the plane.

This was about the time of the Falklands war in 1982 and we thought we were going for sure. Everyone was really positive, and we all wanted it so much – well I know I did. I'm still disappointed that we did not make it there as we were so ready for the Falklands. Instead and I am sure at the last minute, the news came that we were off to Belize instead. We were disappointed, but hey, it was a new challenge.

Another achievement for me in Colchester was learning to drive. This was done by three or four of us in a Land Rover, with an instructor, constantly roaming the streets of the town on a daily basis. However, a good squaddie cannot perform without breakfast, so that was always the first stop, at a little café just outside of town towards Marks Tey. The driving was relentless, day and sometimes night, but wouldn't you know it, I passed first time, with a proper three-point turn included – in fact I hit the kerb doing that, and thought I had failed anyway, so I just carried on. The examiner, a Sergeant Major, said it was not a bad drive at all, but he warned me not to turn into a boy racer, start with a small-engine car and work my way up. I was chuffed to NAAFI breaks to have passed, and I couldn't wait to get my first car, which was a Volvo 340.

While in Colchester I had been told by Kev B that I would make a good boxer. Well, OK then, why not give it a go? Let me tell you what a great sport I think boxing is. I enjoyed learning the art of boxing and for a late starter in the boxing game, I achieved more than I had imagined. If you have boxed, you know what I mean, the training hurts and the fitness is immense to say the least, but I was hooked from the start. I was dedicated from the beginning and I gave it my all. In the Army there are inter-company bouts, and I started there. I learned from some fantastic boxers, but Winston B taught me from the beginning, and we spent months in the old gym in Colchester, training almost every day. In the Army, they expect you to train eight hours a day every day, but that's not possible, you just get stale and lose interest in boxing. If you change the routine daily and do not overdo the training, it works better.

Not only did I box for the battalion, we also boxed for Colchester ABC, whose gym we used to use most weeks. I remember our trainer, Corporal Dave N, was a great motivator, but he was also a hard taskmaster. He made us train hard, but he made it almost enjoyable, and he was a great trainer. Each member of the team would learn from the others, and of course some had experience before joining the Army, so they had good boxing knowledge. We had some great boxers in our team, because yes, in the Army boxing is a team sport, not an individual one. However, when you step into that ring, you are very much alone. My first fight was a step into the unknown but again, through experience, I reached a higher standard. You only get that from dedication and hard work in the gym. As I learned, I got better and more confident. To be honest, boxing changes your outlook, your attitude and the way you treat people in my own personal opinion. You need to control your aggression in the ring, because if you lose your temper, you will lose the fight. It is certainly a good life-learning curve, at least it was for me. It also, in my opinion, bought out the best in me and changed me into a more confident person.

I had some great fights. In the Army team matches consist of nine bouts at different weight categories from featherweight through to heavyweight. I can't remember them all, but I think it was featherweight, bantamweight, lightweight, light welterweight, welterweight, middleweight, light heavyweight and heavyweight, plus a couple of in-between weights I cannot remember.

One of my stand-out achievements was that the Battalion made it through to the semi-finals of the Army Boxing Cup and we were to fight at Chelsea

Barracks against a team of the Scots Guards. This was not long after the terrible bomb placed by the IRA which killed both horses and soldiers. The semi went ahead, and I was up against this Guardsman who must have been seven foot tall. Holy shit, I thought, how do I go about this one? Well as my old trainer Dave will tell you, 'slip a punch and get in close', which is exactly what I did through most of the fight, and I won comfortably on a points decision. This was when I was at my best in boxing. I still love the sport and it is only recently I have had to cut it down due to a back problem, but I still like to work the punch bag at least once a week, if I am still able to.

Yes, they were great days when I was boxing and it is true, the Army loves a sportsman and they'll provide you with the equipment if you want to carry on the sport representing the Army or even yourself. The bad news is that, because I dedicated so much time to boxing, my military career stalled and suffered, and I was left behind when it came to moving up the ranks. It was my own decision, so I have no regrets. But it cost me personally, as for all those years I had been a full-time professional soldier and I let it slip. We were in the boxing team, but for about five months of the year, instead of learning to be a better soldier so I could move up to section commander and get my Corporal rank, I instead dedicated my time to boxing and any spare time was spent on fitness. But bloody hell I was fit!

We used to run at least ten miles around the Colchester area every morning, and this was just for the warm-up, then it was into the gym for circuit training for at least two hours. I have to applaud our trainer Dave N, because he varied the circuits almost every session so that none of us were bored with the same routine. As I stated previously, if you keep on doing the same thing it is boring, and you lose interest, which is not good.

After our run we would head down to the running track and continue with sprint sessions. This running and sprinting is for the legwork, to keep the legs strong, even for those of us with not too much meat on the leg, and believe me, it worked. So, the running part of training is most important. I know that three 3-minute rounds doesn't seem a longtime, but believe me when I tell you that when you are in the ring, it most certainly is. You need that strength in your legs.

Usually, after the sprint sessions, it is back to the

gym for bag-work and learning the art of boxing by using the bags, shadow boxing, skipping and one- to-one training. We used to learn from the more experienced boxers in our group. And of course, sparring. I used to love the sparring, as we would start first, with the lowest weight class, and then move up to the heavyweights. After completing a one-minute round with each boxer, you certainly needed some time out. Starting with the lower weights, I had to be fast and sharp, because these guys were as quick to the punch as I was, but once you spar with the bigger guys, it is great because you do not have to pull your punches and you can hit hard, which gives you a great workout. We certainly gave it our all. Once you step into that ring you are all alone, but the mindset is to work the other guy out, outmanoeuvre him, and once you decide to throw a combination of punches, you'd better throw them, or it is too late.

I think I am right in describing boxing as a chess game in the ring, because it's all about which move to make and when to make it. I certainly enjoyed my boxing days and not only within the battalion but also when we boxed for Colchester ABC, as we trained with the civilian club quite often. We used to attend civilian bouts and would get matched with a boxer of the same level and make fights that way, which was good experience, and as always, practice makes perfect.

I fought at Featherweight, which I believe was up to 8st 13¾ lb, and sometimes I would struggle to make the weight for the official weigh-in, so I would head off to the Embassy Club in Colchester for the sauna. I would be sitting there, eight stone and dripping wet, next to some big fat business man who looked at me as if to say, 'why would you be wanting to lose weight?' But it was needs must, if I didn't make the weight then no fight.

On one occasion again I struggled to lose the last couple of pounds, but this time I did something different. Any of us who needed to shed a couple of pounds would put on one layer of clothing, then make a top and bottom from black bin liners, add another couple of layers of clothing, go into the shower room, turn the heat to maximum and skip or shadow box off the remaining fat! Bloody hard work, believe me, but it did the trick.

I would encourage anyone to try boxing. It's a great way to keep fit and although it's an individual sport in most cases, as a team sport it is also good, because you have team mates to cheer you on and you train and learn together, learning from each other. It's the perfect sport for the Army. I still enjoy watching the boxing on TV, and of course try to keep up with the big fights. And as I already stated, I still try to work out with the bag and keep at least a little of my fitness, even at almost sixty years of age. My dream job would have been to set up and run a little boxing club in my own area, but alas, it was not meant to be. I think two of the lads from our old battalion team did just that, setting up and running a club in Colchester. Well done to them.

I got married while stationed here, and we lived in a flat in married quarters about a mile or so from camp, in Ebony Close. I went back there a few years ago when I was in the area doing deliveries and had a 45-minute break due, so I headed roughly to where I thought it was. I got straight to it pretty much, pulled up and was chatting to a local resident (a squaddie's wife) and we were talking about the time we were there. Those were the days for sure!

Anyway, I was heading into camp all dressed for the day, in barrack dress, I think. There was a stretch that was quite open, and it was chucking it down. This civvy bus drove past and soaked me from head to foot. I swear if I had caught up with the driver, I would have given him a quick combination of wallops to the head! Still I managed to make it on parade on time and dry. You just got on with it, because it meant something. Out in Civvy Street it doesn't mean that much.

So yes, I loved every minute of doing our job in Colchester. As I write I can't wait to get back there in May for the reunion, but I'll deal with reunions later.

There was always time for a little 'skiving' whilst we were in Colchester. I always remember how Paddy C and I loved to play snooker. While we were having a recce of the various buildings around our camp, we came across a single room with a plush snooker table, with chairs around each side, perfect for us. We kept this to ourselves as we very often could not get on the tables in the usual snooker room as it was always busy, and I thought we could use this one instead. I shit you not, we would get up to our snooker room just after NAAFI break and lock ourselves in there until four in the afternoon, and I reckon we got away with this at least once a week. No one has ever known about this until now. Let me tell you, we had some cracking frames of snooker in there, and for a change, we never got caught! We must have played 25 frames a day on some occasions. Well Paddy my old friend, we certainly got away with that one. I can't remember why we stopped, probably because we got posted out to Belize or one of the other tours. Great memories. I must say you can never beat the Army system, but you can bend it a little, if you are clever enough, or willing to take the risk. You'll be in deep shit if you get caught though!

The routine at Colchester carried on, with daily training schedules, a different subject to deal with, remembering all operational procedures, cleaning of weapons and equipment, guard duties, more refresher lessons on the things we hadn't done for some time. We also had our free time to enjoy, at the weekend especially, but no one day was ever the same.

Then along came our next posting, which was a real change.

CHAPTER 7

Kenya, 1980

Was this for real? I was going to Kenya, Africa! I had to pinch myself. Can you imagine? These days you could probably jump on Easy Jet and get there for thirty quid, but back in the 1980s the only people who could afford to go to Africa on holiday were either rich or celebrities. I think it was one of those exchanges – we went over there and some of the Kenyan Army came over to the UK.

So, there we were stationed on the outskirts of Mombasa – actually, if I recall correctly it was one of those giant marquees that the Army have which can sleep a whole company. It was a massive marquee with electric lighting running through. I remember one of the lads, ginger haired, of course, as white as a sheet, got sunburnt badly on the shoulders and as they were erecting the cables and wiring up the place one of the cables, must have been a good two inches thick, fell onto the blisters on his shoulders, and he let out a screech of some description! The blister just popped and the slime from it spurted out in all directions. Thankfully we had our medics with us, so we soon had him patched up and ready for action again. But that was a painful introduction to the need to be careful in the sun!

We were all taught the effects of sunburn, and more so how to avoid it happening, but we felt sorry for the fair-skinned guys who had to be extra aware. There were always going to be some who got caught out – it happened to me on one occasion and I learnt my lesson. I remember having to do a run with full kit and the yoke part of the webbing was rubbing badly on my sunburnt shoulders. When you're carrying 60lb of kit on your back in 40-degree heat there is nothing worse than to have the 'yoke' (shoulder straps) digging into sunburnt shoulders, that was really sore! Definitely controlled suntan sessions from then on.

If you do happen to get sunburn the Army treat it as a self-inflicted wound – you were taught and you did not learn. You have to deal with it and soldier on. After a few weeks your body adapts and acclimatises to the heat and before long any spare time is spent topping up the tan, controlled of course, do not lay out there after midday for sure, but who wants to get back home looking as white as they did before they left? Anyway, once we were settled in we all got used to the heat.

But anyway, who cares about sunburn? This was Africa. It wasn't a bad set-up to be honest. Everything we needed was on camp and it was all rather laid back. I do believe we trained with some of the Kenyan Army, just doing the basics – patrolling techniques, camouflage, all the normal stuff.

A couple of things stick in my mind from that tour. Firstly, our camp was situated in quite an open area and we had the local kids around mainly scrounging biscuits from our ration packs, and begging for dollars. The other was the way they lived, in mud huts basically. The view in the picture pages is much like the actual place we were situated - just picture an Army marquee in the background and that was home for the next six weeks or so. They did let us take a look inside – it was quite impressive, and we imagined they would keep warm at night and out of the sun during the day.

The stores were a few hundred yards away near a small rocky area – bad idea, because a group of the local baboon population would come around the front to distract our attention, while several others would be at the back raiding our stores, stealing everything in sight – very clever. To solve the problem, we had to do 'stags' and have sentries around the clock to keep watch and ward off the intruders. We had all seen the funny side of their game, but mind you some of those big baboons would rip your arm off. So, we did not get too close.

The place was amazing, with the scenery, the animals and the people. We played football with the local Masai warriors, and it was some game – they played in their bare feet! They also used to jump incredibly high, as if in a trance-like state, which was fantastic to watch. Imagine seeing this for real – it was unheard of back in the 1980s.

I also recall a trip out to the Equator, and most of us had a picture taken there, just to prove you had actually stood there. Unfortunately, the picture has been lost along the way. It was a truly amazing place to visit and it will stick in my mind forever.

I bought my mother two carvings of Masai warriors, because in every country I was posted to I had brought her a doll in the national costume. I never knew what happened to them when she passed away in the late nineties, possibly one of my two sisters may have acquired them. She always had the warriors on display, and any time I or my brother Richard came home on leave, she would always feed and water us just as she had done when we were kids. We used to take her for nights out down the local pubs in Kettering. We had a cracking night once, when me and a couple of the lads came on leave – we had a heavy party weekend and stayed for a couple of nights. Then we moved up to Leicester for the next session – great times. My stepfather Brian also enjoyed it. As I've said before, Mum did the best for us, and brought us up as best she could, so we used to love to spoil her when we came home.

Reunions

As I mentioned earlier our reunions are fantastic, because you meet friends and comrades you have not seen in a long, long time. This one came about because I wanted some replacement medals I had lost. My current partner and common law wife (she will love that), Delilah, had got me my medals for Christmas and it started the whole ball rolling. She was amazed on receiving them that the Army had my name, rank and serial number on record so they could readily verify me as a veteran. She was amazing, to be honest, and as excited as I was, I reckon. Also, I must include Lottie, as she helped with it all too. I was over the moon to receive them from her on Christmas Day 2012.

With our new-found knowledge we got onto the reunion site and booked up for Norwich (2015). Also, we got onto Facebook and found out all we needed to know. It was good for me at this point, as I was getting fed up with the same old crap day in and day out. Yes, the girls really made me happy and I have never thanked them for it, so thank you ladies! But I was so grateful for their help – if only they knew what it meant to me. It brought back a lot of memories, stories, life or death events, old faces, comradeship, and if I am honest it was a little too much for me take in. For instance, on arriving at the said reunion in Norwich, I spotted Jim Glover, and as we met, he said, "You were my section commander when I joined the Battalion, and it made me very proud". At the end of the night, the emotion of the whole event and meeting again with friends and comrades after thirty-five or forty years had affected me emotionally, and I am not ashamed to say I shed a tear. It was all too much in one night.

When we dress for a reunion, we have a veterans' dress code. This is light grey or black trousers, white shirt, with regimental tie and dark blue suit jacket, with Royal Anglian crest, and finally topped off with our battalion beret with cap-badge, plus medals on some occasions. So, I had a dress rehearsal to make sure my gear looked good, a sort of kit inspection before the actual event, and I will never forget the look on Delilah's face. She just stared at the medals and it seemed that she suddenly realised how much it meant to me. That was a great memory. Thank you babe.

At the first reunion in Norwich I remember that after a couple of drinks, I needed to go to the toilet, so having grabbed the attention of Ian C, I introduced him to Delilah and said, "Look after her for a while, I need the loo." With that I shot off to the toilet, where quite a few of us had assembled. We were chatting away about the old times and it must have been forty-five minutes before I returned to Delilah, but no problem, Ian had told her the story of the time he was on patrol and was blown fifty yards up the street on his backside from the force of the explosion from a nearby lamp-post which had badly injured one of our officers in Northern Ireland. He told us the only thing that bothered him was that the QM (quartermaster) wanted to know how he was he was going to pay for his denims, which of course had a gaping hole in them. Thank you, Ian for reliving that one with us. Delilah was amazed.

The reunions are great for telling old stories, or as we say, "pull up a sandbag and I'll tell you a story." They were a great get-together with old comrades and the whole family, and they just keep getting better.

I must also mention the Regimental Day at Duxford. On entering there, the current serving soldiers who greeted us called us all 'sir'. Total respect to them and thanks for respecting us. They do so because they know what it is to serve and put your life on the line for your country.

We're on to our third reunion shortly (2016) and I'm going 'home' to Colchester for this one. I'm hoping to meet up with a few more comrades from the Battalion. The more I get involved the more I can remember, and I'm starting to put a few more names to all of the faces.

The Colchester reunion has been and gone and again another great time was had by all. I must say from a personal point of view that I loved 'Colly' when we were stationed there, but I must say I did not like the town at all now. It had become way too overcrowded for my liking and the High Street was just a stream of people heading in all directions, not how I remembered it at all. However, I know that several from our Battalion have made it their home, so who am I to judge? To be honest our old barracks have all been demolished now, and only a part of the main gate fence is left standing, so our old 'home' has gone. However, I did find the time to visit the Army married quarters at Ebony Close. One of the locals told me that some of the estate is still owned by the MOD, but most have now been sold privately. At one time I could see myself going 'home' to Colchester, but alas no more. I guess I have become used to the quiet life.

Yes, another good reunion and it was good to see the old place, although it has changed so much. I missed the Northampton one in 2017 but I made it to the 2018 one, in Leicester. Unfortunately 2019 was cancelled, which is a shame, as it would have felt like going home.

CHAPTER 8

Belize, 1982

I absolutely loved Belize. It was hot, humid and great for fitness, as we were never off the five-a-side football pitch morning, noon and night. I was well into my fitness regime here and it's perfect for this as you never stop sweating. One of my favourite postings, for sure.

I remember stepping off the plane on the first day and how the humidity hit us. After five minutes we were all sweating profusely. We had been to Cyprus, and that was a warm breeze compared to this place, the humidity was so high. My memories of the camps aren't too clear though. I know Rideau was one of them and I think it was the main camp for the duration, but I have fond memories of Treetops, which was a camp/observation point built right on the top of a plateau and overlooking the border with Guatemala, perfect for watching the 'enemy'.

The good old RAF would drop us off at the Treetops site by Wessex helicopter, and it was a fantastic ride. The getting there was an easy landing, but on the way out the pilot would clear the edge of the plateau and suddenly dive nose first into the jungle, a fantastic rush believe me. You have got to admire those pilots, all great guys. We used to stand on the roof four abreast at Treetops and mark the pilots' landing skills, displaying boards as if in a competition, six out of ten, nine out of ten etc. The pilots would just give us the one-fingered salute back!

I must say that Treetops was and is one of my favourite places. We were dropped off for one or possibly two weeks at a time, then carried out jungle patrols, observing all the time. We also had to keep the camp in a reasonable state, and I remember once we had to refill and replace a sandbag wall. It was a pain in the arse job, however we got on with it as usual. As I did a shovel full of dirt a colourful bootlace-sized snake stuck its head out of the dirt to have a go at me. I duly splatted it and chopped it in half with my trusty shovel. When I showed it to one of the locals, we were told that if it had bitten me, I would have had about five minutes to live! I think it was called a coral snake, like the one in the picture here, one of the most venomous in Belize.

At the other end of the scale, we were doing a regular jungle/border patrol and as we passed under a tree one of my patrol stopped me and pointed out to me that wrapped around the branch of a tree, we had just passed under was a massive snake. It must have been five or six feet long and as thick as my thigh, and I had never even seen it. It was a scary fucking place I tell you.

I enjoyed the patrolling though, and you learned how to look after yourself and your unit in extreme heat conditions whilst being able to do the job, which really was patrolling the border and peacekeeping. Unfortunately, I do not have any pictures from my time there, or only one or two – the rest of these were taken from another source.

I remember that during the patrols along the border, we would chat to the 'enemy' at various points and try as best we could to communicate. We would exchange cigarettes for girlie magazines and such things, or swap chocolate from our ration packs. I got a pair of Guatemalan combat trousers by doing this on one patrol. One guy took a liking to my SLR, but he soon understood that no fucking way was I passing that through the fence! We got on well and we kept the softly-softly approach, as it seemed to keep everyone calm. They were doing their job, just as we were.

I was sad to leave, as I loved the place, so with that in mind I treated myself to a large bottle of Blue Label Smirnoff to take back to Blighty. Not a big deal now, but back then that was a pretty potent bottle of vodka.

On my way back to the accommodation, I took time out and sat next to the five-a-side football pitch, just relaxing. Before long a couple of the guys came over. 'What you got there Smudge?' After about five minutes a small gathering had formed, with plastic cups and a bottle of coke. My bottle was passed around, and I didn't mind – what a great way to give the place a send-off. I'm pretty sure we were bladdered that evening. I still want to know who the culprits were.

On a more serious note, I have to mention that we were posted here with the Falklands War on our minds, because just before we came, we all thought we were going to the Falklands. We were ready to go, believe me, and we were that close, but at the last minute the Royal Marines were sent in our place. I have since found out that the reason we did not go was because we were not anti-tank trained! (mechanised). On a personal note, and I believe I speak for most of the lads, we wanted to go and were at our peak, and we were so ready for it. I will say to the Marines who went, we were there with you every step of the way and you all did a fucking superb job. We would have loved to stand beside you fellas. There were some unnecessary fatalities, but there were always going to be fatalities. On the whole it was a great job, professionally done.

The military also found out that the kit we carried was next to useless and seriously out-dated, so a change of kit and modernisation was desperately required, from the boots up!

I believe the Battalion were posted there shortly after I left, so I missed out on that one.

July 13 2017 was a sad day, because that was when we attended the funeral of Roy Holohan. It was a great shock to all of us to lose another Pompadour so completely out of the blue. At the last reunion we had shared a cab to the venue and Roy and his lovely wife Lynne were telling us how they were now just going to get on with life. Roy had suffered more than most, a couple of cancer scares, but he had kicked its butt. Also there were family issues, pretty much like most of us, I guess. But he looked so well, and as you can see from the photograph he was in good form. We are going to miss you, Hooligan. You were a top man and a great fellow Pompadour. RIP buddy.

Well we certainly gave Roy a great send off and the service was very moving, especially for the family – his elder brother gave a great speech. He will be sadly missed.

CHAPTER 9

USA, 1984

We were still based at Colchester, and our next little jaunt out was to the good old US of A. Fort Lewis is a US military facility located 9.1 miles (14.6 km) south-southwest of Tacoma, Washington, under the jurisdiction of the United States Army Joint Base Garrison, Joint Base Lewis-McChord. It was merged with the United States Air Force's McChord Air Force Base on February 1, 2010 into a Joint Base as a result of the Base Realignment and Closure Commission recommendations of 2005.

Joint Base Lewis-McChord is a training and

mobilization centre for all services and is the only army power-projection base west of the Rocky Mountains. Its geographic location provides rapid access to the deep-water ports of Tacoma, Olympia and Seattle for deploying equipment. Units can be deployed from McChord Field, and individuals and small groups can also use nearby Sea-Tac Airport. The strategic location of the base provides Air Force units with the ability to conduct combat and humanitarian airlift with the C-17 Globemaster III.

Yes, this was another great posting. I think I am correct in saying it was one of those exchange deals, where we went over there, and a company came over to the UK. It was only a six-week exchange I think, but I loved every minute. Pretty much all that I can remember is the vastness of the place, how everything was so much bigger. .

We were based at Fort Worth, Seattle, in a massive complex and layout. Apparently, this was the place where the film 'An Officer and A Gentleman' was filmed. They certainly know how to look after their troops there. The equivalent to our own NAAFI, it was called the CX, and it was like a superstore even compared to today's standards. You could buy pretty much anything there.

We trained with some of them and as I have already mentioned we shared the ranges. They were fascinated by the SMG (Sub-Machine Gun) and the SLR, and could not believe how heavy it was compared to the M16 which we got our hands on in Belize.

I remember us all going out on the town for a few beers, and finding that they were very strict, and you had to have ID or no drink. We were all in one bar and one of the 'oldies', I can't remember who, did not have ID. They just would not serve him, so I said I would have a pitcher of beer and give the kid a Coke! I must have only looked about fifteen. We found the place a little too dull for our excited souls, so we decided to head off somewhere else and asked the bartender for some directions. He said we should go a couple of blocks down the road and hang a left for another bar. So off we went, but after about fifteen minutes walking, we were getting a little naffed off. We had not realised that a couple of blocks was like two or three miles I think we called a cab in the end.

I also remember having a day on the ranges there. We were zeroing our weapons (SLRs) and as usual firing groups of five to ten rounds or so, then adjusting sights up or down as required and then another grouping of five to ten rounds. Anyway, along came a platoon of American squaddies with their M16s. They all lined up and emptied whatever ammo they had at a big circular target, ceased fire, slung the weapons and off they went. Peace through superior firepower, I guess! And half of them probably never hit the bloody target at all.

The Americans really liked the British Army, and to be honest we all got on with each other well. It helped that there was no language barrier but mind you they do have some words that mean exactly the wrong thing in English. For example, on one of our nights on the town one of our section asked the barmaid for a jug of beer. 'Say what?' was the reply from the aforementioned barmaid, who gave him a rather awkward look. The explanation was that jug means a breast in the States, so in effect he had asked for a tit of beer. No wonder he received the evil eye. The situation was sorted with the minimum of fuss. Some of the Rangers looked pretty mean to us and it would not have been good to upset our hosts. Mind you, they did not want to upset us either!

The equipment and resources they had, the size of the barracks, housing accommodation, vehicles, weapons and numbers of troops even back then were mighty impressive, but despite all of that I personally thought we made the better soldiers. I do believe our training was harder, stricter and more strenuous and detailed than theirs. However, having left the Army before the Iraq and Gulf War all kicked off, I never had the privilege of serving alongside our greatest ally. I'm sure the new breed will be able to tell me, but what I can tell you is they were great to work with, they were professional and hard-working, and like us, they were immaculately turned out. And they loved the Brits!

They also loved our weapons, and I especially remember the SMG was a favourite of theirs. One ranger wanted to swap his M16 for my SMG, and I would have gone for it, but I think trying to hand in my M16 to the armoury at the end of the day would have been a little too difficult to get away with. It would have been glasshouse time for sure! I think I know now why they liked it so much – I guess it reminded them of the WW2 weapons, and to be honest it was a little dated, however in the SMG's defence, it was as I recall an effective and most excellent weapon used in the correct environment. Close Quarter fighting to be precise.

At this point that I must mention that here in the USA is where I began to go downhill. A big mate of mine, Titch W, a PTI and one of the best, pulled me to one side and said he had some bad news.

So, let me put this into perspective. Here was I on my way and doing well, loving the job and my rank, looking to move upwards, and happily married to M. Life was great. What could possibly go wrong?

Well the news was that apparently as soon as we got on the plane for the States my missus had had another guy round. I was gutted to say the least. I took it badly and of course took to the drink. I was angry and could not believe it. Thanks to CSM S for allowing me a little time to gather my thoughts and let off some anger, because for what I said to him he could have locked me up for a long time. I have always respected the military etiquette, but I lost it a little that day. Thank you again, sir.

Anyway, without dragging it on it was doomed from that day on. Yes, there is a families officer and his staff who assist you with guidance, but not for us I am afraid. How could you ever trust someone again who would do that?

The situation was also confirmed by my brother Richard, who popped in to the flat at Colchester a few times as he was driving his lorry in the area. One time he told me he popped in and there were bodies all over the flat, lying in the hallway and on the sofa. It was party time again and she was in bed with another fella. We tried to keep it together for our daughter's sake, but it did not work out.

Finally, on this matter, yes, I did have an affair with a married woman during our turbulent time, but by then we were already finished as a couple. That did not work out well either and I suffered for my woes, so it was all MY fault! We tried to stick it out and lasted until the early part of the posting to Germany, but the end was sour when it came, and emptied the house and my bank account. However, I did not expect it to still be going on forty years after the event, when my ex was slagging off my family and trying to ruin my current relationship. Unfortunately, our daughter was also poisoned against me.

No names are required here and suffice it to say the finger was always pointed at the wrong person. Some people who are still around today, take note. I am guilty of some terrible things, and I will take them to my grave. End of story.

Let us move on with the military. So, despite the

upheaval in my career, I really did enjoy my time in the States. Unfortunately, I have never been back, so I must add it to my bucket list.

My career was now on the downward slope and I found it difficult to keep soldiering on, but it was what I had been taught. I did not want to give up, I loved my job and I so regret the way it ended. If I had the chance to do it all again I would. Let me tell you the Army is a fantastic place to be, but you have to live by certain rules and regulations. Sure, you can maybe bend and stretch them a little, but if you try to cut corners or not do as you should, you will be found out. For the moment though, despite the anger, hurt and pain that this problem had caused, I needed to get on with it and keep going.

Only recently I have found out that I actually left Recce Platoon and had gone to Mortar Platoon during my last couple of years, if it wasn't for one man I would have given up long before, so thanks Polly my friend, I will always be in your debt. I will also take this opportunity to apologise to people who believed in me and whose respect I had earned and then sadly let them down. Fuck it I am naming names, so apologies to Monty, Brian H, Billy E, Dave N, Gap D, Titch W (bad news bearer), Maj S, CSM

S, Bob Mac, plus all of those whom I served with or who served under me, and all those I taught, knew and respected.

Despite all of this, during this difficult time, the good always outweighed the bad. My proudest time was before I left and screwed up at Brecon, on the Section Commanders' Course. Prior to the course I needed the experience of my own section, so I was given the rank of Acting Corporal, and had my own Section, my own 'lads' to look after, train, encourage, reward and keep safe. Let me tell you, there is nothing better than earning the respect of people whom it was your duty to look out for. A rule that served me well was, never ask anyone to do anything that you could not do yourself or have done. You have to command respect, not demand it.

I will never forget the guys in my section; John Har, John M, Roy, Mike L, John Hew, Tony G, Paul S... forgive me fellas, I cannot for the life of me remember you all.

I also remember, though for the life of me I have no dates available, taking my section out for the first time on exercise one time. Where we were I do not know, or if I did know it escapes me, but as a section we all have our given jobs to do and of course, as I was the new Section Commander on the block, my section inevitably always ended up with the crap jobs that were needed to keep the position in running order. This meant digging latrines or 'shitpits', stag duties, keeping the platoon area secure with a rotating two hours on duty and four hours off, and other trivial tasks. It was no problem doing this, but after a couple or three days of it my guys got a little aggravated and to be honest, proper pissed off, and asked why we were always doing the same menial tasks. I agreed with them and said I would sort it at the next Platoon O group. I guess that possibly Brian H, Gap D will recall that at the O group I said that my section were a little pissed off with the same crap and so was I, and said to the Platoon Commander, a Second Lieutenant, could he give it to one of the other sections, as my guys and of course me were pissed off with it. Also, the fact that I and my section also needed the patrolling and other special duties to be able to learn and practise our in-the-field training. So, after that day, no more shit shovelling for my guys as we had done our share. They were pleased that I had spoken up for them and so was I. The other two well experienced NCOs had also realised I was not going to be shat on anymore. Another valuable lesson learned – stand up for yourself and your men, they will respect you for it. It was a big testing moment for me too, you must understand, being the new boy on the block. But respect given to the other two NCOs and our officer for backing me up. My wording really put the point across, methinks. I think I said 'my guys are not just shit shovellers, and just because I am a new Section Commander shouldn't mean we get all the piss poor jobs, so don't fuck with me, and that seemed to have done the trick. I must say that every Section Commander and Platoon Commander did help me. There is so much to learn as a new Section Commander.

Once you have attained the rank of Lance Corporal it seems the Army likes to keep you learning fast. In most cases, shortly after getting that rank you will be put forward for the Section Commanders' course at Brecon to attain the rank of Corporal. Bear in mind that we were now stationed in Germany, and it costs a substantial amount to send soldiers away for these courses. I suppose because you are fresh and have done well then it makes sense to keep the momentum going and push you on to the next step.

So, there I was, being shipped back to Blighty to

attend my next course. I never complained – why would I? – and well, to be honest, I was good to go, as well as the responsibility that goes with the job. You also earn a little more in the wage packet. Win-win situation.

Briefly, I need to mention the Section Commanders' course at Brecon. I arrived ready to go and looking forward to the challenge, I so wanted to do well, as I had done in earning my first step on the way to climbing the ranks, and as most of my old mates had already done. For me to come first on that course was really pleasing, and I knew that I could do well here at Brecon too.

Basically, all I can remember is arriving, getting settled in at the barracks, meeting everyone from the different Regiments, all chatting about our current postings and generally finding our way around the place. The first couple of days went well. It was going to be tough, but I was more than capable, and we all worked hard over the first few days. When we got to the weekend, some decided to stay in camp and revise while others shot off in their own direction, possibly to head home for a last hoorah before the hard work began. I decided to stick around and check out the local pubs in town, so a small group of five or six of us headed to the town for a few well-earned beers.

This was where it all started to go wrong. I cannot remember exactly what caused the argument, but I was being a little loud and one of the others told me to shut my mouth – bad move. Anyway, we were ready for a fight, but nothing came of it – not until we had actually got back to camp. Then as I walked through the barrack room door, he began giving abuse, and it was like a red rag to a bull. I hit him with a combination of punches, thinking I had it sorted, but he then stood up somehow and actually round-house kicked me in the head, just connecting above my eye. We were both in a bloody mess and we both called a truce and agreed that we had better get up to the medical centre.

Funnily enough, after such a nasty fight, we actually helped each other to get ourselves blood-soaked to the med centre. We realised our error and blamed the demon drink, and that was that. We were a mess the next morning, and our squad instructor said we had to go straight to the training area, but we had no time, after another visit to the medical centre, to get our equipment or weapons. It was my own doing, but once I mouthed off at the instructor and refused to carry on until I had my equipment, he told me to return to camp!

We were doomed. Well I was anyway. The following morning, we both had to parade at the Camp Commander's office, marched in by the RSM, and told that we had both been kicked off the course and were to return to our units, immediately. My own CO was not a happy man.

That was the start of my decline, and I regret it to this day. If only I had stayed in camp and revised as I had planned, but it is too late now. I did apologise to the CO and I did not lose my Lance Corporal rank, but I did not feel very good about myself. Not only had I let my own high standards slip, I had let down my guys, my Battalion and all of the fantastic people who had helped me to get there in the first instance. I am only forty years late, but apologies to all. I still feel bad about it after all this time, because these things stay with you as a soldier. I hope a comrade or two can understand what I mean, and no doubt you still also suffer now as I do.

But what is done is done. I would love to go back and change it but is not possible so have to live with it, with regrets.

Our next posting was to be Germany (BAOR, British Army of the Rhine) for two years.

CHAPTER 10

Germany, 1984

So it was goodbye Colchester, hello Germany and the Cold War. This was a permanent move, so the whole Battalion had to be packed up and moved to our destination, Elizabeth Barracks, Minden.

Put simply, this is like moving to a new house in civilian life. It's stressful and a pain in the butt, we packed up as best we could for our first time, and I must tell you, though some of my comrades may disagree, that the Army is not too bad at moving a fully operational Battalion to another country on a permanent basis, even though it's a logistical nightmare.

This is a brief description of our roll here. The BAOR had four main elements:

a. Main Force was 1 BR Corps at Bielefeld.

b. British Rear Combat Zone in Düsseldorf, which was to re-supply the fighting formations.

c. British Communication Zone at Emblem, Belgium, tasked to receive reinforcements from GB and to co-ordinate onwards to BR Corps.

d. The Berlin Infantry Brigade, some 3,000 strong and under the control of Allied Control Council at Berlin.

Total manpower was between 60-75,000 troops commanded by a four-star General at Rheindalen.

The British Army of The Rhine was the main element of the British Army based in West Germany from the end of the Second World War until 1994, tasked with being prepared for counter-aggressive operations by the Soviet Union and Warsaw Pact armoured forces.

At the end of World War Two the British Army was so drastically reduced in manpower that the Former British Rhine Army was down to only two Divisions, the 7th Armoured Division and the 2nd

Infantry Division, both based in former Wehrmacht barracks located in Lower Saxony and Nordrhein Westfalia. They were replaced by the Armoured Division in 1950 and 6 Armoured Division in 1952, forming one British Corps part of NATO Northern Army Group Nothag. They were restructured and re-equipped with new weapons.

Although not strictly classified as an operational duty, we were the main defence against attack from the Soviet and Warsaw Pact countries at the time of deployment.

I must say that this was another one of my favourite postings. Even though my career was spiralling downwards I really did enjoy Germany, as there was plenty to do and all areas were open to everyone. Unfortunately, I missed out on the chance to visit one of the old concentration camps – the guys who did said it had been an unforgettable experience. Maybe one day. Again, I will add it the bucket list.

I especially liked the training and the job we were there to undertake, which was basically to wait for the 'Red Russkies' to come trampling through Germany and onwards.

I loved to be in the field, and loved the mud, cold,

rain, ice, jungle, deserts, plains and valleys, digging six-foot trenches to live in and just basically being out there. However, I could never understand the lads who volunteered for Norway. Get real for fuck's sake! I don't mind getting cold, but that was stupid cold.

I was still married when we got to Minden and we were given a very nice three-bed house surrounded by Staff Sergeants and WO2. I had my Company Commander, Major Steele, to thank for that. To be honest, I was very lucky to have a good rapport with him, as he very often let me off light when possibly I could have been locked up. I met up with him probably about thirty-five years later at the Swan in Market Harborough, and still addressed him as sir! A truly great officer and very well respected, as all were in the Battalion. Unfortunately, I have not seen him since, although I live near to Market Harborough.

Germany was one of the best postings of that time. However, as we arrived that year, the overseas allowance had been reduced drastically. They had had to cut it back as there were private soldiers driving around in top of the range BMWs and suchlike exotic vehicles. They had been able to pay for them in cash, after saving for a short period of time. But hey, why not? Anyway, as I already stated, things were not so extravagant for us, but we lived and budgeted quite well despite the loss.

It took some time to get used to the language and most of us had a stab at learning it, even if it was just to order a beer and a bratwurst and chips. We settled in to life here quickly – you have to adapt to wherever you are posted, and this place was no different.

This was a real turning point for me. I had found out the truth about my wife in the USA, and once the trust has gone it is over. We hung on for as long as possible, but it was no good. So, we separated, and I moved back to the barracks.

After the fiasco of handing over the married quarter it was back to the barracks, and I found myself bunked up with a great friend, Mick P ('Polly'). We hit it off very well and were soon best of friends. Mick saved me and helped me through the bad times. But the end was soon to be and even now, after all of this time, I do regret the wrong decision I made at that time.

Army life went on, as it does. It does not stop because you have had a bad time and been kicked in the teeth by some people, you dust yourself down, grit your teeth and get on with the job at hand. Mick informed me only recently that I had in fact left somewhere and been transferred to Mortar Platoon at this time, not the other way around. Not being able to remember is a terrible thing to live with.

Not to dwell, I must tell the best story of my friend Mick P. My first car in Germany was a Volvo 343, a decent motor, but I was in the process of selling so I had it parked up in camp and was not using it. One night whilst I was out Mick had received the bad news that his father had passed away, so to drown his sorrows and probably to hurt himself, he 'nicked' my car, and absolutely paralysed with drink, he crashed it into Minden Bridge. The car was a write off and he was lucky to be alive. Volvos are a strong make of car and if it had been any other make my friend would have perished that day.

He was in the ambulance coming into camp, and I happened to be at the guardroom when he arrived. He was crying. 'I am so sorry Smudge.' I said, 'fuck the car mate, as long as you are OK.' It was only a chunk of metal after all.

The worst part of the story is that it was parked at the camp gates, in a crumpled mess, to remind everyone of the dangers of drink driving. I had to walk past my car every day. I was gutted, but so glad my friend was still with us. He had to pay for it though!

I remember on another occasion that we had our trenches dug by the engineers. They were perfect, with a main fire trench and two sleeping bays, with wriggly tin walls and pickets to hold them in place, fantastic. At night as I got into my maggot (sleeping bag) I had tied a candle in a tin on the side of the trench, armed with a mug of tea and mess tin of stew, followed by AB biscuits and a well-earned ciggy, with a Sven Hassel paperback to read to boot. Luxury! A hell of a lot easier than digging them yourself, that is for sure.

On another occasion I remember we had dug in with several houses to the rear of our position. We must have been on the edge of the training area, as about 50 metres or so behind us was a row of houses. This position was one of the best we had ever built, a big trench and perfect, created by shovel this time, and after the final touches of camouflage were added it was the perfect position. It was barely visible from the front, though we had perfect vision for our arc of fire. A main battle tank could have rolled over this trench and we would have been safe.

The locals came out and brought us drinks and cakes, a nice gesture we thought. Mostly they tolerated us in their country, though some of the older German people did not like at us at all.

The total weight of mortar equipment a section carries, with .22 rounds, is 168lb, which when divided among a three-man crew equates to 56lb per man, plus his personal equipment of 30lb, so that's 86lb per man total.

To continue, the Battalion soon settled in and I finally got my wish of joining Recce Platoon. I had to keep badgering a guy named Billy Eke, Colour Sergeant, and the Platoon Sergeant, for Recce. I knew him quite well from the rifle companies and virtually begged him to get me in.

I'm not sure which was my favourite job, Rifleman/Lance Corporal in a section, mortar man (did a little time there too, in Milan Platoon, for the briefest of time), but it has got to be Recce Platoon. To join Recce Platoon, you had to have done at least three years minimum. This was the cream of the Battalion and just the best job. Our Scimitars took us everywhere, but the Rifle Companies sometimes still had to use the good old DMS and TAB into position.

In the 'new modern' Army we were now mechanised, so we had the Scimitar FRV, a truly great piece of equipment for its time. I believe it served the guys well during the Falklands War too.

Rifle companies were also mechanised using the good old F432 APC. This was a purpose- built recce vehicle, fast, light, highly manoeuvrable 10-tonne tracked vehicle armed with the 30mm Rarden cannon, and with a crew of three, driver, gunner and commander.

Once the Battalion had been called out on the parade square, all in their pre-arranged places, rifle companies, heavy weapons, mortars, Milan and rear echelon, equipment checked, ammunition issued, camouflage cream applied, if people were out of camp then MPs were sent out to round them up. Was it the real deal or another practice/exercise?

As Recce Platoon we were first out the main gates, as we were the forward eyes for the Battalion and would report back directly and only to the CO. It gets the adrenalin going just to write about it now, I remember it so well.

So, it was all out training and back to basics really, equipment checks regularly, training and more training so that when the call came, we were ready to deploy.

The routine went on and we settled in again. Germany was such a clean place that you would never find a piece of litter anywhere. I wonder if it's the same today. As I recall there were no run-down buildings or even scruffy cars on the road. Just before we arrived, they lowered the overseas living allowance, although there were still private soldiers driving around in BMWs – we sure missed out on that one.

Just outside of the main gate there were a couple of bars, shops, and barbers, so it was ideal if you didn't fancy the NAAFI for a pint. Yes, all of you Pompadours, the infamous Ecky's Bar, a great place. More on that one later. It was a great camp lay-out. I have never been back there either, but I'm hoping to in the not too distant future. I do believe that some of the older generation were not happy with us being there, but on the whole it was a lovely country. Being in the military, we had strict dress codes and rules for how to present yourself in public places, and that really helps when you're in any foreign country. You are not allowed to bring the Regiment into disrespect through bad behaviour. I also remember that jay-walking was a no go, and it carried an on-the-spot fine of I think 30 Deutschmarks, pissed or not, and that was a tidy sum back then. It's probably £80 now.

Free time was great too, plenty of places to see, you had the freedom to go pretty much anywhere in the country, and more to the point, everything that was needed was close to or within the camp perimeter. The married quarters (pads) were virtually right outside the rear gate. I was still living out of camp for a while anyway, but inevitably the end of my pretend marriage was over. I will never forget the day I moved back to the barracks, I felt a real sense of relief, because the last few years were not nice, I think we alternated week ends off. Almost everyone in the Battalion knew each other's business, let's face it we were a Battalion family living in a confined area, so it was no different from any small town in the UK.

Moving into camp was fantastic for me at this point, as I needed it. However not everything was rosy to start with as I had to clean up the married quarters because the ex-wife had already left. She cleaned the place out of everything and sold the lot to her buddies around the pads. That really didn't bother me that much, but what did is the fact that she also cleaned out my bank account! I have forgotten the Families Officer's name but he was a complete and utter arsehole, another one who pointed the finger at me without first checking the facts. I scrubbed that place from top to bottom several times, but it was never good enough for him. He issued me with a rather large bill for nothing really. If I ever catch up with him, even now, I will not be held responsible for my actions. There is still fight in the old dog yet. He will get a combination, if I can still produce one! I finally got the prick out of the way and got on with it.

At the time I was still into my boxing, but the soldiering was taking a back seat. I always loved the fitness even without the boxing, and I still loved my football too.

This was the time it all started to go wrong, and I turned to the 'best friend in the bottom of a glass'. Any free time now I was always in the mess or out in Ecky's Bar sinking a few. Don't get me wrong, there was a drinking culture in the Army back then, but we could all sink five or six pints and still be on parade the next day at 0500hrs good to go.

CHAPTER 11

Exercise Lionheart

On or around the 3rd of September 1984 there was another call-out to test us out, but this time we were actually deployed. Yes, this was the beginning of Exercise Lionheart.

Lionheart comprised two interlinked exercises, Full Flow and Spearpoint, the former a deployment through the Rear Combat Zone and the latter a field training exercise for 1(BR) Corps. It involved 131,565 UK personnel, regular, reserve and Territorial Army, the largest exercise since the end of WWII. A total of 290 flights from the UK transported

32,000 personnel. This initial air movement was followed with 150 sailings across the North Sea and English Channel using civilian ferries. The sea routes carried 23,600 personnel with 14,000 vehicles and trailers. 750 main battle tanks were involved and most crossings over the Rhine were carried out with combat bridging, based on the assumption that all civilian bridges had been destroyed. 1(BR) Corps were deployed with 3th and 4th Armoured Divisions and 1st Infantry Division.

Providing the opposition (orange forces) were, 6,300 German (1 Panzer-Grenadier Brigade), 3,500 Dutch (41st Armoured Brigade), 3,400 American (1st Armoured Brigade) and 165 Commonwealth personnel (from Australia, New Zealand and Canada).

Lionheart was the first time US forces had operated in Europe with their new M1 Abrams MBT and M2 Bradley combat vehicles. The newly re-formed 5th Airborne Brigade also formed a second opposition group, joined by elements of the Life Guards and 10th Gurkha Rifles. 13,000 RAF personnel were involved, deploying Harriers and the newly introduced Tornado aircraft.

It was the first opportunity to conduct a major

exercise with Challenger 1 main battle tanks, Saxon and tracked Rapier. The Warrior Mechanised Infantry Combat Vehicle, which was still in early development, was also introduced.

Unfortunately, there were fatalities, three in total, and there were also seven people seriously injured, but considering the amount of men and machinery that were deployed this was inevitable.

A quick note that you can still view videos on You Tube and it's well worth a look to see how things have changed. Here is the link to one of the first video/reports on Exercise Lionheart, copy and paste https://youtu.be/KU-qmHYXosQ into your browser and take a look back at what we accomplished, although most of the footage is about the rear echelon bodies and the TA that flew or shipped out from the UK.

So away we go, and as I have previously mentioned, being Recce Platoon, we were first out of the camp gates. This time it felt different from the normal short trip out and back. The adrenaline was pumping, and we were really looking forward to at least showing what we could do on the battlefield under simulated conditions. Every squaddie will tell you that some exercises are the same old routine, however we had to treat them all as reality because God forbid, if it was for real then you had to be ready.

With an umpire close at hand – they wore white arm-bands so they were easily recognised – we had to do everything by the book (follow standard operating procedures) as we always did. We were professional soldiers. All equipment was checked, vehicles were checked, weapons oiled and good to go. If you had forgot something, too bad, we were on our way. I will never forget the eight Scimitars rolling out of the camp gates, a great sight. It was raining as usual if I recall, but who cares?

Incorporated into this exercise was live firing, which is something different from the usual blank rounds, and it also gave the whole deployment more realism, as this is how it would be, so soon after deployment we were given co-ordinates for an RV point. This was the live firing ranges.

Let me tell you that this was impressive. Firstly, we had the A10 Tank busters fly over and take out some of the targets (old tank hulls and assorted soft targets, Land Rovers and troops. The noise and firepower from an A10 is awesome. Our Scimitar was fitted with a 30mm Rarden cannon and we could get quite a few rounds down quickly, but the Warthog had a 30mm Gatling gun fitted, so it created a complete hail of 30mm shells all impacting the target at the same time, and it's unstoppable. I do not think there is any tank that could survive such an impact. I will never forget the noise for sure. Check it out on You Tube, it is well worth a look.

Then it was our turn to take out any left-over targets, firing and manoeuvring. The Scimitar was fantastic. I was the driver, and getting the guys into position for targeting took some practice. The smell of cordite and the adrenaline pumping made it an unforgettable experience. OK, the 'enemy' were not firing back at us, but all the same it remains one of those 'once in a lifetime' achievements fulfilled.

As we moved on to the next phase, the Companies would all come through the live firing phase and cleared up whatever we had missed, boots on the ground, so that all phases were practised for real, ie Company and Section orders right down to each individual soldier. We had all done this before in training. It was their turn.

As the rifle companies cleared up, we then moved further forward to carry out reconnaissance on the Orange forces. We would find the high ground and basically wait for the enemy to come into view, watching, waiting and reporting any movements.

In simulated battle conditions we moved quickly and covered plenty of ground in the first day. At our first RV we 'cammed up' and got into the usual routine for the night, sentries out, preparation of equipment, ready to move in a second.

On to the second day and we were now approaching the Orange Forces area and were ready to be attacked. Not so – again, it was back to the night routine again.

The next morning when we were woken up by the night sentries, we found ourselves in a small copse on some high ground. It was dense with foliage and plenty of trees around for cover, and we were located deep in the middle. We had got set up just before dusk with camouflage nets, sentries worked out and food and a brew, and we settled for the night, a chilly night but not too bad. It was a perfect spot with undulating ground, just slightly higher in the direction of the enemy threat. There were open rolling hills, with several small wooded areas dotted around, and visibility was good.

However, virtually just after we had opened our eyes the ground started shaking with the rumbling of enemy tanks as they passed by our position. We acted fast, got back into our vehicles and stayed put, not a sound. As the vehicles passed, we counted them and used tank recognition so we could relay the information back. However, we soon realised we were surrounded in every direction!

No panic. Our commander, Sgt Billy E, was calling in to the CO with all the numbers, vehicle types, direction etc. In all of this time, say two hours, not one of the vehicles, and there must have been 40 or more heavy tanks, had seen us, and I shit you not these massive Panzers were about 15 feet from our position passing by the copse. If one of them had chosen to come through the middle, we'd have been screwed. Luckily, they did not.

However, we could not stay in our position for much longer. In a real-life situation we would probably have tried to sneak out under cover of darkness. But this being a military exercise the umpires were asking what we were going to do, as we had given so much information back to Callsign Nine (our Commanding Officer) and needed an escape route.

I think I am right in saying that we were told to create as much havoc as possible and take out as many enemy tanks as we could. In other words, a suicide mission!

We made our plans. Sgt E and all the vehicle commanders, Steve N, Kevin M and I forget the other one, set us up for our final fling. First it was time to remove our cam nets and get all equipment stashed away. Then we had to load up with ammunition (thunderflashes in our case, to simulate us firing the 20mm cannon). There were all manner of grenades, green, red and even yellow, some for cover, some for simulating firing and some for smoke cover.

We had split into two groups if I remember correctly, and we charged out with all guns blazing. The Scimitar was a highly manoeuvrable vehicle, and we used it to great effect that day.

Four vehicles went one way and four the other, throwing thunderflashes and smoke grenades as we hurtled along, and with that the tanks lined up on top of the hill simulated firing back. Utter chaos.

When we arrived at the bottom of the hill the umpire stopped us, and we discussed the outcome. I think he gave us three kills, but we were wiped out! A little harsh we thought.

But unbeknown to us, about seventy or so men of our Battalion were at the bottom of the hill playing 'dead', which meant sitting around and having a brew. As we were charging out from the copse, they were all cheering and shouting like crazy. We had really given them a good show.

In a real-life situation we would never have moved from that position, unless compromised, and if we had, we probably would have sabotaged the vehicles and left on foot to go on and recce another area, causing chaos to assist the Battalion. It was not to be. That was us out of the exercise and now 'dead' along with our other brothers in arms.

I believe I am right in saying that in a real attack, if it ever happened, the top brass figured our life expectancy in the field was six minutes. We had done well to 'survive'. A great experience, but over all too quick. We were back to camp after the end of the exercise, and back to the usual routine.

I believe the MOD have issued a BAOR Medal recently and I was debating whether to get one. It is not a ceremonial one, so it cannot be worn with our others. After a while and much deliberation, the conclusion was that yes, it may not have been a 'live' operation, but we were there just in case the old 'Cold War' kicked off and we would have been frontline if it had. So I believe we earned that right.

In fact, the British Army are stationed all over the world in various operations, but we should not be handing out medals for any old tour or posting. We were in Germany for a reason. And once again we did our job to our usual professional standard, as always. I believe there is a new Cold War now, so good luck to the guys on that one.

This was the last hurrah for me. From this point on I really cannot remember what went wrong, but I had started to give up as a soldier and I had decided it was time for me to leave the Army. I think I just lost the plot completely. The part I can remember is going on CO's Orders and saying to him I wanted out, especially after the Section Commanders' course had gone so wrong. His response was that I was a fool and had the world at my feet. He said all of the guys I had joined with were now Sergeants and pushing on, while I was still only a Lance Corporal. He also said that if I had carried on soldiering instead of giving it up for my boxing, that might have helped. He finally stated that he would let me go, but he gave me 21 days 'nick' to seriously think about it, as he thought it was the wrong decision by me.

He was so right. I regret the decision to this day, and I have had to live with that.

My first few days in the Battalion Guardroom were hard. All of the Provosts and Sergeant L knew me and knew I had served 10 years already. They also knew I was super-fit and no amount of drill, running or sit ups would bother me. After a few days they left me inside, to clean the cells or something.

One time while serving my time the Provost Sergeant, John L, came to my cell one day and said 'Look, why don't you stay in?' He suggested I could become a member of his Provost staff and just sign for one more year, and he would keep me on the right track. It was tempting, but I said no to that too. If only.

It felt strange leaving and it was hard for me to adapt to civilian life, in fact I don't think I ever have done really. I still miss it after all this time. However I have a son called Ethan, who I think is going to follow in my footsteps and join. I taught him early, and he loved the chance to get out in the dirt. I will not discourage him, in fact I encourage him as much as possible, no matter how mad the world has become just recently. He definitely has the Army mentality, and by the time this little book venture of mine is completed, he should be at IJLB Harrogate, or almost anyway. I am relieved to hear the same routine goes on today in the new modern Army. He has a lot to look forward to.

Just recently via the social media, and having found my old Pompadour family, Ethan and I went along to our Regimental Gathering at Duxford, and luckily enough the lads currently serving brought along some of the equipment. Wow! They have clothing for all weather conditions, and everything seems more compact compared to our old 58 Pattern webbing and backpack. As I remember, right from the early days of training this webbing would be uncomfortable and digging in to your side, and after another few miles of 'tabbing' it would be rubbing somewhere else. When you had to attach the large pack/backpack to the yoke it pulled the back down and your waist belt would be pulled up to your chin. It would be digging in to your shoulders as well, and inevitably it would slip off the padded section. Hey, we got through it though, what pain? And the next day, and the next etc…

However, I did notice that the new body armour is very heavy, though thankfully the new recruits wear it in stages. In my day we just had the 'flak' jacket in Northern Ireland, which would probably stop a 9mm round from about 30metres but not much else.

Yes, I must say that the new modern Army is moving with the times in the equipment department. The other pleasing thing is that looking back to the way we were trained some 40 years ago, the training is the same as it was back then, and why not? 'If it aint broke don't fix it' springs to mind.

I have added to my bucket list something that I really need to do, and that is to spend a day or two with one of the Battalions, whether it be in the UK or at one of the overseas postings, preferably Cyprus, just to see for myself and to meet some of the men, and now women, whose duty it is to keep us safe in our beds at night. As we did some forty years before.

Northern Ireland revisited

I am working from the office these days, but a couple of years back, whilst I was still able-bodied enough to drive, a delivery came up for Ireland. I was offered the job and of course I said yes, not just for nostalgic reasons but also because it would be a change from the normal motorway network in England and a change of scenery, and I was curious.

I was fine until I drove off the ferry, and I could see Belfast approaching. As I got nearer the streets seemed recognisable and I could see exactly where certain events had happened some 35 years previously. I am not ashamed to say there was a tear in my eye. It was like patrolling the streets. The fear came back, and I felt scared for the first time in a long time. I even had goosebumps. I soon got to grips with it and was muttering to myself 'wake up you fool, it's different now, there is peace where once there was hatred, you are a civilian, and nobody will recognise you'. I did not want to be a civilian, I wanted my protection back, the lads, the 'flak jacket' my rifle. The hairs on the back of my neck were tingling. I was visibly shaking, and I had to pull over. 'Get a grip of yourself, Smudge!' I inwardly shouted to myself. After ten minutes or so, I had calmed down and got my act together, and everything was 'normal' again.

I think it was just the initial shock of being there, so many memories, good and bad. By the time my delivery was done I had missed the next ferry, so I had a couple of hours to spare, and I drove to Holywood, home of Palace Barracks – it was still used as an Army base, I believe. I felt so much better. I parked up and strolled around the town I had known so well back then, when we had been based there for 18 months in 1978, and now I felt safe. I recalled when some of us had popped out of camp on our rest period for a beer down the local pub. Well, almost safe.

I made the next ferry back and had to endure another night, so I took a room for the night in one of the motorway services, as it was too far to drive all the way back. This helped really, as I needed the time to reflect. I still do, as do many others I have no doubt. I doubt I will be going back again.

We did our duty a long time ago now. We were the guardians, we were professional soldiers, we kept our country safe and every single one of us was proud to do so. When we meet up now on our annual reunions, the numbers are slowly dwindling away. We always relive some part of one such event, for example a shooting, a riot or and IED attack (improvised explosive device) or another story such as the time we were outwitted by that bunch of baboons in Kenya that stole our food from the kitchen store. The laughter, the tears and the comradeship will never stop. It does not matter whether you are a rich accountant or you sweep roads for the local council, we are always, as we were then, equal. And in it together.

We still have respect for each other. We do not talk about the bad things, because they are personal and remain that way. Not even those closest to us know about those, and it will stay that way forever, and rightly so. We just look each other in the eye and say nothing.

We have still a dress code for veterans, trousers, blazer, shirt and tie, with or sometimes without a beret, and we still wear our medals with pride.

Though it's not likely to be a best seller, I just wanted to get my story down in writing. The memory is fading now and the days when we were kings are long gone, but if you have ever served and picked up a weapon for your country, you will know what it feels like, and hopefully you will relate to some of the contents of this book. Maybe it will stir a memory, or just bring a smile to your face, and if so then that's great. If one of my sons happens to pick an old tattered copy up and a little smile appears, that would be great too.

All we ask is for a little respect, as we have certainly earned it. Actually, a little more of that, along with manners, empathy and common decency in today's crazy, fast-moving world would not go a miss.

The Government should also utilise our experience, and put it to effect by way of recruitment, where we are able to pass on our knowledge to new soldiers. At present, as previously mentioned, my son has applied, and to be perfectly honest, the recruiting process is dreadful. Instead of passing it on to some civilian company, why not employ some of the veterans to look after the new breed? We have all had the experience, and we would definitely not let recruits wait with no information or contact for weeks, with no encouragement or updates to the progress of their application, it truly is disgusting. I have heard that many who have applied have actually given up, because the process takes far too long, and these guys and gals just find another job, and who can blame them? Yes, we do understand the medical scrutineering side of things, but the whole process takes too long. At the time of writing I do indeed intend to look further into this matter and maybe write a few letters to those concerned. Time will tell, maybe the red tape and higher echelon people will sit up and take note.

We could also be used in the local cadet training,

again passing on our knowledge and helping the younger lads who wish to join. Yes, there has been debate about the claim that joining at 16 is too young, but that's utter rubbish in my eyes. If you take a year to absorb all the information needed whilst still carrying on with your education, then that has to be better than cramming the training into 16 weeks or whatever it may be now. It never did me or my comrades, who all attended IJLB Folkestone, any harm. I found it easier this way, and you have the chance to leave if it is not for you. Or they could use us in another capacity within barracks – there are plenty of jobs we could do there, from stores jobs to armoury, issuing weapons. Not sour grapes, I'm just trying to make a point. Apart from my reunions and phone calls to old comrades, that is it for me. I loved every minute of serving.

CHAPTER 12

Civvy Street

We are now in July 2018, and my son Ethan is about to follow in his Dad's footsteps and will be going to join the new Modern British Army very soon – he is currently awaiting his assessment day. He is so ready, and luckily for him he has more insight into the Army now than we had back then. The fitness standard alone required to join would be difficult for some to achieve, you have to run a mile and a half in 12 minutes! But he is currently flying around in under ten, good lad. We are similar in build and he, like me, loves the physical aspect of the job. He is destined for greater things in the military I am certain, but his journey is just beginning, and I wish him the best of luck. Although his application is held up (because he had a migraine once) He will never give up.

This all started when he was maybe five or six years old, and I used to take him 'up the woods'. In fact it was like our own private training area, where we would learn all the skills, camouflage and concealment, patrol techniques, making camp etc etc, covering pretty much most 'in the field' training, and I kid you not, he is a natural. He is well on the way now, by the time I have this completed he will probably be a Lance Jack (Lance Corporal).

We recently spoke about the new modern equipment mentioned earlier. He certainly knows how tough it will be, but I am certain he will be ready for all of those challenges ahead, because he has it already built in.

I have settled now, not far from where life began for me, in Desborough, approximately five miles from my old hometown of Rothwell in Northamptonshire. There is me, my partner Delilah, who I love so much, her daughter Lottie, and our two cats Sissy and Sox. Ethan is over every couple of weeks, but not for much longer, as he hopes to be following in the old man's footsteps. I'm sure I gave him the bug to join, it must be in his DNA. Good luck son and enjoy the ride.

I've also changed my name, to Eagle instead of Smith. Everyone knows me as Smudge 37 or L/Cpl Smith. I have a job as a Transport Planner, for a small company based in Wellingborough with ten full-time staff and four of those are our full-time drivers. We all get on with the job in hand, and all in all it's not a bad place to be. The work can be quite hectic at times, but we roll with it and prioritise as we go through the day. I'm still in full-time employment at the moment. The back problem, a degenerative spine, is worsening day by day, but I'm still able to keep going. Morphine is easing the pain at the minute, and by the time this book goes into print I should know whether there is an operation available to make the back pain more bearable. Failing that it is spinal injections. Either is fine by me, so long as one of them is successful.

Delilah is a hard-working carer in a nursing home and looking to move back into office type work – they all deserve medals by the way. However, she is looking to getting a management position at the home, or a complete change in direction. We have discussed it and I'm sure she will decide shortly. Good luck in whatever you choose babe. Lottie has now moved back home. She has a great job in the local pharmacy, and as mentioned earlier Ethan will be following his old Dad in about six months' time. I figure, like almost everyone else, that we budget and work to live, but to be honest, I have never been more contented.

I'm motoring on to 60 years old now and life is not bad at all. It's hard not being able to do the things you used to do, because the brain and heart say yes, but the body says a definite no. However, I am well looked after and in comparison, with some of the heartache my old comrades have suffered, I am not doing too badly. I get free prescriptions, and it is not at all bad.

There is not one day goes by without the Army popping up somewhere, through social media for instance, one of the guys posting about a holiday or some old pictures he found from back in the day, a memory just out of the blue. Or something on the national news, even a reminder whilst walking in town. Or just in my head, because you never forget. And why would we? We were proud, well trained and ready to die for our country.

The training we received, and some of the dreadful things we had to endure, never go away, and it's still useful to this day. If I feel down, which happens quite often now, all I have to do is conjure up one of the situations we were put in, and I have so many to choose from, and hey, life is not so bad after all. Some of the memories make me sad and tearful, but mostly I smile at those treasured memories. Believe me, it is something very special to carry with you always.

Back then it worked for us and it still works today, definitely – the best trained army is the British Army. I still miss it, always will, and missed it for a few years until, through social media, I was able to contact some of my old comrades. I and am happy that I never lost touch with my old life completely. I'm looking forward to the next reunion, in May 2019.

I hope you have enjoyed my short memoir of my 10 or so years in the Army in the seventies and eighties.

I must make special mention of the following guys who assisted, changed, helped, trained, inspired, encouraged or generally were truly great soldiers and/or friends. In no particular order: Monty B, Polly, Bob M, Billy E, Brian H, Fred B, Mark R. (Scratch), Gap, Dave N, Tony G, Steve S, Pete H, Jimmy M, Titch W, A Steele, Spud Y, Andy C, Kev M, Steve Nev... so many names in fact. Let me just say to everyone I served with, you all know who you are, so thank you one and all. All the fours, the Pompadours - up the Old Red Rooster!

Abbreviations and military terms

66mm: Small anti-tank weapon
84mm Carl Gustav: Anti-tank weapon
ACC: Army Cadet Corps
AWOL: Absent Without Leave
Brick: Four-man unit (NI)
Choggy shop: on-camp café
CO: Officer Commanding (Battalion)
Cpl: Corporal
CSM: Company Sergeant Major
FIBUA: Fighting in Built-Up Areas
Flak jacket: Protection Jacket (N. Ireland)
GPMG: General Purpose Machine Gun
Grots: Underwear/boxers

IED: Improvised explosive device
IJLB: Infantry Junior Leaders' Battalion
JIB: Junior Infantryman's Battalion
L/Cpl: Lance Corporal
MP: Military Police
NAAFI: Navy, Army, Air Force Institute
NBC: Nuclear/Biological/Chemical
NCO: Non-Commissioned Officer
Nick: Prison (in barracks)
OC: Officer Commanding (Company)
Pig: 1-Tonne armoured vehicle (N. Ireland)
PTI: Physical Training Instructor
RCT: Royal Corps of Transport
RP: Regimental Policeman
RPs: Restriction of Privileges
RSM: Regimental Sergeant Major
RTB: Return to Base
Sgt: Sergeant
SLR: Self Loading Rifle
SMG: Sub-Machine Gun
SOPs: Standard Operating Procedure
TAB: Tactical Approach to Battle
Thunderflash: Stick-like pyrotechnic
Tin Lid: steel helmet
VCP: Vehicle Check Point

Printed in Great Britain
by Amazon